I Am The Love Of My Life

HORACIO JONES

I AM THE LOVE OF MY LIFE

DISCLAIMER AND/OR LEGAL NOTICES

The information presented herein represents the view of the author as of the date of publication. Due to the rate at which conditions change, the author reserves the right to alter and update his opinion based on new conditions. This book is a work of personal perspective.

This material is general dating perspective only and is not intended to be a substitute for professional medical or psychological advice. This book is for entertainment purposes and enlightenment. This book contains sexually explicit material and profanity and is not intended for persons under the age of eighteen (18).

ACKNOWLEDGMENTS

My Solitude

I AM THE LOVE OF MY LIFE

*Welcome to the SECOND book written by
Horacio Jones. If you find yourself questioning
your love for "self", look at the way you allow
people to love you. More often than not, how we
allow others to treat us will expose much about
ourselves because we are responsible for what
we tolerate. Be receptive to the idea that you
enabled bullshit behavior by being faithful to it.*

This book will tell you what you already know...

In this book, "*I Am The Love Of My Life*", I give you my opinions and my own understandings. I used personal experience and the experiences from love ones and so many other people who are in successful relationships and from those who are in the most disastrous relationships. The purpose is to continue my journey <u>with</u> you to self-love. The best way to read this book is by having an opened mind. Understand that each chapter is its own piece of a journal. Each chapter stands alone. There is no particular order. So, after each section, take a deep breath… we are healing. We are becoming the love of our lives…

Contents

Take Your Own Advice

When I sit back and consider the most important events in my past, the significant pieces of my current life, and my future goals, the main theme is appreciating different perspectives of relationships. I don't believe that any of us have the answers to cure our generation of dating. But, what I value is being able to listen to or read about someone else's story and relate to it; learn from it, and grow with it. That helps me evaluate myself and my choices. I believe that the best thing we all can do is share knowledge, evaluate ourselves and then TAKE OUR OWN ADVICE.

Have you ever given your best friend advice about dating, but when you were in that same situation, you rejected your own advice? We give advice all the damn time to our friends, family, even strangers—but the one person we never seem to listen to is ourselves. I think I know exactly why: When things get hectic, the easiest thing to do is fall back and let someone else take the wheel. So, we ask around to see what others would do in our situations. However, what happens after getting everyone else's opinion? We **still** have to analyze what they think we should do. We still have to take what makes sense to us, and abandon what doesn't. We still have to make our own decision based on that collected advice, ANYWAYS.

I try to give advice when I'm asked for it. By now, people already know what kind of answer they're going

6

to get and that's why they come to me in the first place—to hear the hard core truth. I never tell people what they **should** do. I tell them what I would do if I was in that situation. Then I tell them that it's OK to let go, to move on, to leave your ex alone…. Blah, blah, blah, because they want to hear it from someone who isn't going to judge them or make them feel like shit for staying. Ultimately, posts on Instagram are just my opinions about their lives and truths of my own life. I don't have the answers. Take your own advice.

Why Is It So Hard to Take Our Own Advice?

All we have to do is look in the mirror and ask ourselves for advice. After all, who knows us better than, well, us? No one is more deeply mindful of our own situations than we are. No one is more aware of every specific scenario and potential outcome than we are. Therefore, at the end of the day, it's all on us! Take your own advice.

We choose to give out our own advice rather than take our own advice. Why? When someone is crammed and doesn't know what to do, we start freely suggesting solutions—not realizing that that same advice would actually be wonderful for our own situations. When we look at our own lives, we look at it through a small scope, noticing our strengths and limits in extreme detail, maybe even exaggerate a few things. That's why we feel like some advice that we give won't work for our own situations. When we observe others, we perceive just the highlights of their lives. So, it is much easier to throw "you should do this, you should do that" at them because we don't feel responsible for their outcome.

Try this—**my greatest discovery of all time**: The next time someone is trying to decide what to do about who is fucking them over, as you spit out your advice, think to yourself, "Have I ever needed to hear this shit myself?" Wake up! You're giving out advice about what YOU would possibly do in that situation, so when or if you're ever in that situation, why not just take that same advice since you felt sooooo confident that it would work?

When or if we're ever in that situation, we don't take our own advice because we often justify to ourselves why our problems are so different. We think, "my situation is different. They just don't get it." No, it's not **that** different and it's not that they don't get it, it's because we understand it from a different perspective than they do.

Listen to the advice you're giving out to others. If they do not take it, that's cool and fine. But YOU came up with it though. You have no excuse actually. It's YOUR advice. Take your own advice.

It's one thing to give advice to someone else. But, try applying those same recommendations to your own life. Try taking your own medicine and all of a sudden you say "fuck that advice, it's not going to work for me." That is because it's a simple matter of our perspective being switched. It's more personal and serious. It's difficult to be your own love doctor because your emotions are more likely to influence your judgement.

It's easy to assume you know enough of someone else's situation to give them a thought out opinion when your heart isn't on the line. It is the easiest job in the world to throw that "logical" advice at them because you don't have much to lose really, and if that does not work out, you could always blame the other person for not following your advice: "See, I told you so." Or, "you didn't listen to what I was trying to tell you." Take your own advice.

Following your own advice means you have to take up responsibility for whatever happens, and that shit can be the hardest thing in the world when the reality of that advice results in us not being with that specific person anymore. It's easy to talk, but it's walking it, that is the tougher part. Take your own advice.

Be the love
of your life
and one day,

you will

stumble

upon <u>that</u> love

within someone

else.

Horacio Jones

I Am The Love Of My Life

I looked in the mirror... self-love was looking back at me with a blank stare, drowning in tears for being ignored for so many years. I was just there... holding another empty wine glass... "am I drunk?" ... self-love was staring back at me, into my soul.

A thought dawned upon me, self-love has been with me in my darkest hours of my life, but I didn't pay attention. Self-love has been with me in the cloudiest moments of my life and I still didn't pay attention. Self-love was there when I wanted to be love. Self-love was there when I wanted to find someone to love. But, why did I ignore you?

It was because I was looking for reasons to feel wanted and completed **OUTSIDE** of myself. How was I ever going to find what I've been looking for in someone else if I wouldn't take the time to find it within myself? What I REALLY wanted in life was more love and appreciation for myself, no matter what anyone else had thought of me so that if for whatever reason things didn't work out or if I was ever rejected, I would not feel completely empty; I would still feel complete with enough love for myself to keep going. I found that without self-love, I would have still been stuck in poisonous patterns, which would have always been recipes for unhappiness.

12

I truly did not love myself at one point in my life. There was a time in my life where I spent most of my time settling for less than my heart deserved, constantly letting insecurities and fear stop me. I kept sacrificing my worth and dreams; procrastinating; Settling for being called *"damaged"* instead of striving for the life my heart and soul were craving.

I found myself suppressing the depression and dating people to keep me distracted. Situationship after Situationship. I was often the **"side dick":** the boyfriend #2, the guy you call when your boyfriend is acting like an ass and all you want is penis with no strings attached. I was that booty call. It was all fun and games until I realized that I didn't want to share anymore and until I actually started to want someone just for myself.

I wanted my own girlfriend. So, I had decided to let go of the side boyfriend gig in order to make myself available for single women. But, I only attracted the type of women that were good for short term fun and long term drama. My relationships tended to be emotionally abusive, and I allowed them to endure because I was always afraid of disappointing women. I wanted to "prove my worth" and show them that I was the best option for them. My happiness was solely based on what THEY said, what THEY felt, and what THEY did.

I allowed myself to be completely lost in someone without defining who I was as an individual. I merged with them. I became them. So without them, I felt like I was no one for a very long time. I needed to figure out what was REALLY missing from my life. Was it money? Was it sex? Was it a girlfriend? What the hell was this void?

Looking For Love In Other People:

I first tried finding it in relationships or MORE Situationships. I "freely" gave love that was not satisfied with any reciprocity and it usually resulted in resentment. For me, the desire to be loved—to the level that it made me feel appreciated instead of lonely—was very challenging. I had betrayed myself and I wanted to "save" people and felt that maybe the challenge of proving my worth would distract me from my own internal chaos and keep me from having to feel lonely. I gave my all without asking much in return. I thought that making them happy would make me happy. I gave money. I gave attention. I gave, gave, gave and what happened was that I forced people away by giving TOO MUCH all because I was insecure and lacking of self-love.

"Too much of anything is bad for you." Too many attempts at dates. Too many gifts. Too many apologies. Too much complaining... I was over doing everything and trying to compensate for the lack of self-love. I thought that someone else's love would fill the voids. I forced myself to "prove my worth" when they ALREADY knew my worth. I basically tried shoving it down their throats. "I deserve this, I deserve that."

14

I AM THE LOVE OF MY LIFE

Lesson: Looking For Love In Other People:

(1) When you try to fill the self-love void by loving someone else rather than trying to love yourself first, you become codependent and desperate. We will find ourselves making lots of sacrifices for our partner's happiness, even while not getting much in return. Instead of finding wholeness within ourselves, we show unhealthy clinginess and our sense of purpose in life wraps around making exaggerated sacrifices to satisfy someone else's needs because we feel that we aren't capable of being happy without them. We will do anything to keep THEM happy even when it keeps us unhappy.

(2) There is a fine line between loving someone unconditionally, and loving for reciprocity. For me, I used to think when I loved someone why SHOULDN'T they reciprocate? However, I've concluded that when I love someone with the expectation that something HAS to be given in return, this is loving from an insecure place. But, after a while, too much giving and not enough receiving is toxic and it was time to give myself what I felt like I was lacking. It was the expectation that made the love an act of insecurity. From then on, I began to choose to love myself first.

(3) I was so insecure and jealous because I wanted them to love me in the same way that I wanted to be loved. I was giving them what I wanted in return. I was often disappointed by my expectations for reciprocity

and in the end I felt betrayed by my own self. I had to realize: they didn't love like I wanted them too and If I wanted that love, I had to **give that shit to my damn self.**

Looking For Acceptance As A "Player":

I made the good-guy-to-fuckboy transition. "Fuck hoes, get money." I dated women, I lied to have sex, and didn't return calls. I dragged women on for months manipulating them into believing that all of that sex and cooked meals was going to earn them a committed relationship with that "potential" man that they wanted me to be. Sometimes, multiple women in a week and was only getting praise from the homies. I'm not saying that I had game like **that**, but I had enough to get at one or two pretty girls and maybe 6 or 7 half decent women per semester to "slide to the dorm room." That actually made me feel **good** about myself. I felt like I had discovered a new purpose and gained respect.

The sad part was that I was attracting more women just as I stopped caring and they wanted to "fix me" and make me better. How ironic, they were doing things for me that were exactly what I used to do for women: "proving their worth." I knew that these women were good women and deserved way better than my lies, **dick-hypnotism** and manipulations... and dirty plates left over from their full course "I'm the Wifey type" meals. But, I just didn't want a relationship at the time because I was tired of trying. I had lost **hope**, and I guess I was stealing **it** from them. *Confessions of a fuckboy.*

16

The truth is, I was still looking to be accepted. As a fuckboy, acceptance came in the form of praise from the homies like **"yooo, where the hoes at? You got all the hoes?"** It was a form of respect amongst the **fuckboy culture**: you better have money and you better have hoes or else you're not allowed out with the boys and we're going to clown on you and call you 'gay' if you don't fuck multiple bitches. It was an honor to be the guy who **"gets all of the hoes." Confessions of a fuck boy.**

See, when you are a fuckboy, you don't really care about women's feelings. You don't care too much about people calling you a "male hoe" or a "dog." You don't care about women not wanting to take you seriously. You just care about your money, respect from the fellas and sex from the women who are willing to let you be you.

I just loved to feed my ego. My pride was stroked because I was surrounded by the opposite sex at will. It made me feel good. The pride of being seemingly adored and "liked" by many can really be exhilarating… until you start wanting a real bond with one woman, and you realize that all of that "respect" is fake; destructive.

Lesson: Looking For Acceptance As A "Player":

You have been giving multiple people who probably wouldn't make good parents a chance to be your accidental baby mother/father. Condoms break and some of these people are way too messy.

There is almost no protection against sexually transmitted DEMONS. Being a cheater, compulsive liar and manipulator takes a toll on your soul and can turn you and people you have sex with into monsters.

When you spend years playing games in multiple ways, it's just like any other behavior that gets boring or addictive and damaging over time. After a while, when you keep doing it, it becomes your habit. It becomes a part of your character. Even when you want to change, you don't know how to. You start to feel lame; old news.

You start losing and hurting great people... ones that you actually like and want to keep in your life. You don't know how to keep them because you're so used to pushing them away. You don't know how to be genuine because you're so used to manipulating them.

By constantly cheating and playing games, it becomes such a bad habit that you lose your morals, your values, your consideration of other people involved. So, you get too used to what you are doing and it's not giving you the same pleasure and satisfaction anymore, and you start realizing that what is happening to your life and yourself will take a long time to change.

You are still unhappy because all of your approval comes from outside of you, but your inner demons are eating you up inside. But you fake a smile, fake a life.

Looking For Love In Other Things:

I started to develop an obsessive attitude. First, I became "addicted" to playing video games. I stopped studying, I stopped paying attention to human life and growth, and spent all of my time playing PlayStation for hours and hours. Then I grew out of that stage and became "addicted" to social media. It felt like I couldn't go a day without posting something on Twitter and Facebook. I was looking for things to distract me from my lack of self-love.

Lesson Learned:

Unlike gambling or drugs, video games are not addictive. It is all entertainment and instant gratification, which often leads to more hours of playing. However, unlike actual addiction, choosing not to play video games does not have physical symptoms of withdrawal.

Addiction is relief of a negative feeling (you feel bad if you don't play them); video games reinforce a positive feeling (you feel good when you play them).

This isn't a justification for playing video games for hours on end. It will take a toll on your personal physical health. You can become lazy and abandon responsibilities. It distracts you from taking care of important things. Focusing so much on video games leads to a lack of connection with the people around you. Spending many hours in front of a screen and not enough social interaction can also cause social problems.

19

When it comes to social media addiction, it's all about wanting to feel important and relevant to other people. You want them to know what you look like, what you are eating, who you are dating, what you are thinking etc.

Dear Men Who Messed Up One Too Many Times But Tried Honestly Winning Her Back

The good ones go when you wait too long to change and you get it now. You messed up big time and regret it. You lost her, your lover. Your best friend but you've made a REAL change in your life over the last few years trying to win her back. However, your ex still sees you and treats you like an *"enemy"* or *"evil"* person and reacts to everything you say and do with doubt, pettiness and rage. Even though you've made a real change, not just for her, but for yourself as a man, she *still* doesn't want to forgive you.

The hard truth: Sometimes, you just run out of chances bro. Sometimes, you try to fix your mistakes and bad choices but run out of time. It sucks because you may not have been ready to be the man that she wanted you to be for her or the man who YOU really want to be, but now you *are* ready while there's no guarantee that she will ever take you back. It's hard. You know she deserves better but you want to be the man to give it to her now.

As hard as it may be to accept, moving on — as in it's over, find someone new — is sometimes the only option left when the trust and motivation to work things out has been broken. You're a better man, but possibly for someone else now. You deserve better too. You just had to grow within yourself to realize it. Be strong bro.

I just hope some guy reads this and realizes that even after becoming a better man for himself, it may still not be enough to get her back but it also means he's still deserving of happiness... even if it will be with a new woman.
When a woman walks out of your life... not just any woman, I'm talking about the one that's been trying to hold you down, your best friend... it leaves a huge hole in your heart. Yes, you made bad choices and some mistakes that resulted in losing her but NOW you see how much you needed her. Now you hear her after she stopped speaking to you. This whole time she wanted you to change, it wasn't only for her. She wanted you to do better for yourself as well. And by the time you saw it, she was already gone.

Sometimes, our changes aren't good enough for HER and she don't take us back. That's when we have to accept that maybe all of this time when we thought we were changing for her, we were actually changing to prepare ourselves for someone else. Bless up.

Maybe...
just for now,
it is ***not*** the
time to salvage
old love for and
from anyone else,
but to embrace
love fully,
all for
myself.

Horacio Jones

Maybe it is time
to accept that
I do not have
to search for love
anywhere else;
not when it is
already inscribed
into my being,
my heart,
my soul,
my identity

Horacio Jones

Or maybe…

We can still
spend
the rest of
our lives
loving each
other...

.... just not
together

Horacio Jones

I Want To Change

Dear self, you can change if you want. In theory, you can spend today being the person you want to be. Let's say you want to be a fit person who eats healthy, reads a lot, and avoid poisonous people. Now, you can literally go for a run today, follow that with a healthy meal, two hours of reading AND no checking up on your ex or responding to their bullshit. That can happen today! The problem is, it probably won't happen tomorrow or the day after.

Why? Because change is hard to maintain. Let's be honest here: it's not that it's so hard to eat healthily, or to take a few hours out of your day to read. Or to finally stop replying to people who are just obsessed with the power over you. No, that stuff isn't hard, you can do that stuff right now. However, changing yourself into someone who eats healthily **often**, or reads **OFTEN**, or meets NEW people instead of entertaining old ones – that kind of change is very hard to maintain because it involves changing your lifestyle and consistency.

Wanting to change is only half of the battle. Doing it one time is a small part of the fight. But being committed and consistent will take you to where you want to go. What seems to work best for **ME** is that I have a goal version of myself in mind and started making minor changes in my life. Just small alterations to my lifestyle that wouldn't cause too much chaos with my normal schedule. So, instead of having every meal be a healthy one, I eat just one healthy meal every other day. It isn't always a huge meal, it is usually a simple and easy one. Over time, I have started to eat healthier meals way more often.

Also, instead of reading all day, I cut 15 minutes out of my "social media" time to read something significant. Same thing with jogging; short time limit and distances. When it comes to exes, I put my phone down to find something else to do that is actually productive instead of communicating them. I believe that if we apply this method to everything in our lives where we want to change, without forcing it, we'll turn into the type of people who we want to fall in love with, THEN self-love is so much easier. Just be patient with every change. Increase them when they become comfortable. I hope his perspective helps.

I AM THE LOVE OF MY LIFE

Love yourself more and allow
someone else to love you when
you are afraid... What happens?
You feel BETTER.

Love yourself more and allow
someone else to love you when
you are ANGERY... What happens?
You feel BETTER.

Love yourself more and allow
someone else to love you
when you are feeling HELPLESS...
What happens?
You feel BETTER.

Love yourself more and allow
someone else to love you when
you are LONELY... What happens?
You feel BETTER.

Love yourself more and allow
someone else to love you when
you are JEALOUS... What happens?
You feel BETTER.

Love makes you feel better, all ways, always.

Love Yourself Or No One Else Will?

If you don't love yourself,
how in the hell are you going
to love somebody else?

While I do understand that "damaged" people should learn to love themselves first before attempting to be with other people, there is also the fact that some people are bad at doing it, others are very slow, and some people will never truly know how to. That's just the truth. So, does that mean they have to be alone or that they can't fall in love while being damaged? No. It just means that they still need to work on themselves and that could be done while in a relationship with someone who is very compatible and patient. If you are lucky to fall for someone with endless patience, then you can slowly blossom and learn to love them back the way they want. I don't think most people see it that way though.

We hear it all the time, "If you don't love yourself, how good of a partner can you be? Love yourself or no one else will." I don't even like that damn quote anymore because it is not entirely true. The REAL truth is that someone can still fall in love with you while you're at your worst. They can fall in love with your broken pieces. It may not be a fun experience for either of you, but it is definitely possible. Aren't we all a little damaged and trying to grow within ourselves? Aren't we all work in progress?

Also, you CAN love someone else while you barely love yourself. It has been done. People say "Love yourself

27

or no one else will" because they believe that you can only reflect to a person what you see and think about yourself, and that if you don't love yourself on a fundamental level, you can't convey that love to someone else or, at least, it doesn't come easy. As a result, most people will treat you how you treat yourself and that doesn't feel good at all. However, there are some people who are willing to treat you better than you treat yourself because despite of all of your flaws, they still love you. People can still love you even when you don't love yourself, but loving yourself makes it a lot easier.

I've loved a few people who didn't love themselves. It wasn't always difficult, in fact, it was sometimes easier. I think they needed love more than others. They were seen as vulnerable people who needed saving. At first, it feels good to have someone look to you for help because most people like to feel needed. We like to feel like we could be the missing piece or that we could be the cure to someone else's unhappiness. In certain cases, "damaged" people used my love for themselves as proof that they deserved better from themselves. If someone else could love them, they felt that they could also learn to love themselves.

So, if you don't love yourself, it's not the end of the world yet… I believe that most people don't love themselves, but they find something about themselves to be satisfied about and that gets them through their days. However, we can't ignore the fact that one of the toughest things to do is be with someone who doesn't love themselves.

When you don't love yourself, it's hard to believe anyone else can. You will look for proof of other people's lack of love everywhere, read into everything they say or do, because you "know" deep down there is no way someone could possibly love you if you don't. It's one of the saddest and most hopeless situations you can ever find yourself in, because no one else's love will ever be good enough for you.

If you continue to feel as though something is still missing in yourself, you will most likely rely all on someone else to fill your voids. You will sometimes consider YOUR happiness as solely THEIR responsibility. That is when "saving" you gets out of hand and turns into too much dependency, leaving them feeling less valued for who they are, and more used for what they can do to MAKE YOU happy since you won't make yourself happy. That is never easy for the other person unless you improve.

So, when it comes to loving yourself before loving someone else, my ultimate opinion would be that even though it is possible to date while not loving yourself, you shouldn't. Healthy relationships occur between two people who are comfortable with themselves and each another. Better love only develops after making your own happiness a top priority.

Forcing It

Sometimes, it just happens: there's someone you think is a great person, but that "SPARK" and chemistry factor just isn't there with them. They're nice; they're funny; they're smart; they're not needy or petty. Maybe your friends and family even think that they are dope and are repeatedly warning you about how "the good ones go if you wait too long." But still, you just don't feel "it" for them. You try to force the love, you try to go out on dates, you try to return calls, you try not to be "too busy" but end up losing more feelings and interest until you just give up and let them go. You see, no matter how hard you try, you just can't force that love because it doesn't feel natural, genuine or even unique. It's the same way when you try to love yourself; you can't force it, and maybe that's why it's been so hard to do. If you try to force the love on yourself, it just gets frustrating.

One of the best ways to gain more awareness as to what's going on here is to do a bit of soul-searching. When you're being completely honest with yourself, are there reasons you can identify as to why you're not feeling stronger love for yourself? Maybe you've been hurt and are still unclear about moving on because you still feel as though it was all just your fault. Or maybe there are other unresolved issues from past relationships, even non-romantic ones that you need to address. Maybe you hate your looks, diet, job. You can't force self-love if you don't even like YOU or if you don't appreciate the things that you DO like about YOU. And, of course, it could be that there's simply not enough chemistry with yourself because you're not "your type". That happens. The point is that the more honest you are with yourself, the better you'll be able to figure out what is a good way to change so that you become the type of person who you would WANT to love.

I remember times when walking out was the only option and I still wouldn't take a step. And now that I'm used to taking those steps, it's hard to stop for anyone new

Horacio Jones

How To Start Loving Yourself

Let People Love You

It wasn't until I started to observe how my friends and family loved me that I started to believe that it was possible for me to love myself. These people held me accountable and kept me responsible. They didn't let me spend time depressed alone. It was never easy for anyone involved, but they never gave up. They basically loved me until I started to love myself. So, for those people who are still struggling with loving themselves, getting reassurance and support from a loving partner, friends and family is very important in the healing process. Reminding someone who is struggling with self-acceptance that they deserve to be loved is truly a gift. Accept the gift of genuine love from loved ones.

Treat Yourself Better

Ok, so trying to force the love didn't work out too well. Now what? How can you love yourself?

Start by treating yourself better. The result should be a better version of yourself who you would WANT to love. This does not mean that you should hate your current self, this is inferring that you should strive for bettering who you are: the good and bad. The thing about treating yourself better is that it doesn't always require love. It initially requires commitment, consistency and effort.

For example, if you can clean your bed in the morning, you can clean your head in the morning. Making your bed does not require love, it's not even fun or enjoyable. But you do it anyways because you don't want a junky ass room and you're taught to do so. It's a habit. The result of that habit is a nice looking room that you end up liking and feeling comfortable with. As a result, you make sure to keep it clean because you love your room and who the fuck wants to live in filth anyways? It's a basic example, but you get the message. The point is this, when you "clean your 'self'", you eat better, work out, think positively, remove poisonous people, don't run back, and motivate yourself to work hard, become self-aware, (all ways of treating yourself better) you'll become your own type, unforced, and fall in love with the new version of you.

Eat Better

Now, I shouldn't have to tell you this. I'm not even a health specialist, but we all know damn well we can't possibly love ourselves fully while eating poison every day. Yo, let's take our hard headed asses to a got damn Whole Foods Market and stop playing around with these fast food restaurants. Let's try organic foods or vegetarian places because they have tons of clean healthy foods prepared and ready to go.

There are lots of selections to choose from. The only down side is that they are not cheap. But you get what you pay for and more with healthy food. Those who follow a healthy, well-balanced diet reduce their risk of chronic diseases, lower blood sugar, decrease the risk of Heart Disease and Cancer. Also, they look sexy, feel sexy, and are more often in a better mood with a clear mind. The goal: Eat Better = Look Better + Feel Better and Live Longer.

Workout

So you're sitting at home, and life is passing you by. "Maybe I'll go to the gym today, maybe I'll go for a jog tomorrow" … no, get the hell off of your ass and go do it today. There's such an exhilarating feeling that comes from really getting into "a zone" and staying there (both physically and mentally). Working out burns our excess mental energy which allows us to concentrate better during the day and go to sleep (and stay asleep) at night. It feels good to be "in-shape" and have the energy, strength and stamina to do the things we like. It feels good to LOOK good and sexy.

Balance being key, there's nothing wrong with wanting and maintaining a healthy body-fat-muscle mass. And speaking of fat, we LOVE food…. and exercise is a great way to give us some leeway in eating the bullshit that we love to eat. I believe that working out can help build a highly habit-prone mentality that you will get to a point where it's such a routine that NOT doing it gives you anxiety. The goal: Workout = In Shape + Look Sexy + Feel Sexy + Look Heathy + Feel Healthy.

Love your body with your actions,
or it won't love you back. If you
are careless with it, it will hold
you back, humiliate you, and
even kill you.

Think Positively

What we think will eventually become what we
believe. This is why it is so important that we focus more
on positive thoughts and start saying positive things
about ourselves and compliment ourselves throughout
each and every day. We naturally try to use our gift of
positive thinking and compliments when interacting with
those around us. But, let me ask you this... Do you show
yourself the same consideration?

Bullshit is all around us so don't you think focusing a
little bit of positivity inward would do us some good?
Thinking positively doesn't mean that you are 100% "Ray
Charles" to the bullshit or the reality. A positive person is
not someone who ignores the reality or facts. It is
someone who knows that in any situation, there is always
a lot that we can and can't control, and so it is only wise
to expect the best and put in our best efforts not to trip.
It means that you are very much aware of what the hell is
going on outside, but regardless of all of that, you
CHOOSE to be happy, and don't allow other's opinions,
interactions, situations and negativity to influence you
37

more than you influence yourself.

Motivate Yourself

Look, nothing is going to work if you don't really like doing the work and if you let it keep you from at least trying. If you want to be a better person, how the hell are you going to be a better person if you're always looking for ways around the shit that actually makes you a better person? If you want to be a better relationship partner, there are no short cuts. You have to do what good partners do and create the habits. Not only that, but you have to find a way to actually enjoy the whole process. Otherwise, what's the point? And the motivation to do better and be better isn't always going to come from other people. You're grown, motivate yourself.

I believe that self-motivation is always better than motivation coming from outside, anyways. If you are self-motivated you don't have to look to someone else for motivation every time you need it. Once you find your own purpose, it will fuel you. The only way to motivate myself to work hard is by not thinking about it as hard work. I think about it as part of making myself into who I want to be: a hard-working person. As simple as that.

The "hard" part is choosing and accepting what it is that I have to do consistently. Lord knows that there is a shit load of stuff to do that I KNOW will result in good outcomes for me, but I just don't want to do all of those things. Human nature keeps telling me to look for short cuts to evade the difficulty. But, once I've made the choice to do something, I try not to think so much about how difficult or frustrating the process may be; I just think about how good it might feel to finally get my ass through it, or how proud I would be of myself. I like being the kind of person who is capable of finishing even when the end result isn't all cracked up to what it was supposed to be. At least I pushed myself.

If I fail because I basically don't have a certain talent, luck or enough time and it stops me from being able to achieve, that doesn't mean I'm a failure. But, if I fail because I don't work hard enough, I half-assed it, quit or just because I'm plain lazy, none of which are what I want to be, I can only blame myself; I can't even claim I was beat or not good enough if I didn't try…. And I hate quitting and blaming myself.

I guess at the end of the day, when you need to motivate yourself to take care of business so that you can become the type of person you would WANT to love, it all falls on what your purpose and goals are.

What does purpose mean to you? If you don't know what it is, create it. That will motivate you to make a difference in your life.

Learn

Provide yourself with new skills and arts. Developing skills is one of the most direct and therapeutic ways to boost your self-esteem and positive energy. Cultivate and improve qualities within yourself that you would love in someone else.

Accept Yourself

Fall in love with the new you.

If you ever have trouble feeling love for yourself, know this: Love and acceptance are also actions.

Self-love is not solely about how you feel about yourself. It is also about what you do for yourself. You can love and accept yourself by doing, not just thinking and feeling. Execute deeds of love, and acts of admiration, for your own benefit

easier ~~said~~ ~~than~~ do~~ne!~~

25 ways to learn to love yourself

1. Stop comparing yourself to others.
2. Keep up with your hygiene.
3. Accept yourself as you are, then commit to getting better.
4. Start working out on your own pace. Exercise because it is good for your soul, health and appearance.
5. Strengthen your natural talents and use them.
6. Spend more time with positive people. They recharge you.
7. Spend time alone. You also recharge yourself.
8. Read a book. Write.
9. Research random, but significant things.
10. Spend time outside. Discover a new place to vibe.
11. Let go of the past while being hopeful of the future.
12. Call old friends and family.
13. Let go of attachments that no longer serve you.
14. Buy yourself nice things.
15. Buy someone else something nice.
16. Pick up a new hobby.
17. Save up money and travel somewhere.
18. Laugh.
19. Eat healthy food.
20. Do favors without expecting anything in return.
21. Don't aim to please everyone.
22. Positive self-talk.
23. Get a good amount of sleep.
24. Pray/Meditate.
25. Let someone new love you.

*questions to always ask yourself
when making decisions:*

**1. Will this choice direct me to a
better future, or it will give me a
regretful past?**

**2. Will this choice give me long-
term success or short-term
pleasure?**

**3. Am I fulfilling myself or am I
trying to please "someone else"?**

**4. Am I looking for what's right or
am I looking for what's wrong?**

**5. Will this give me life or drain me
of it?**

**6. Am I going to grow and learn
from this?**

**7. Does this empower or dis-
empower me?**

**8. Is this an act of self-love or self-
sabotage?**

**You will find the right choice. Not
what's easy or hard, but what is
feels right.**

to have a good day

before you get out of bed, think of everyone you're going to come into contact with today.

Think about co-workers, classmates, neighbors and random people around.

Don't leave the house until you can answer this:

"Why am I thankful to see these people today?"

By doing this, you prepare your day for positive interactions.

Undamaged

"**Kintsukuroi** - (n.) (v. phr.) "to repair with gold"; the art of repairing pottery with gold or Silver lacquer and understanding that the piece is more beautiful for having been broken"

Kintsukuroi (keen-tsoo-koo-roy) is the Japanese art of repairing pottery. It is such a dope concept that I randomly stumbled upon one day while being thirsty, double tapping booty pics on Instagram. This picture was on one of those Instagram models' page (she had booking info) and I left a simple comment: "dope." She replied back and asked me what was my take on it. I had a simple explanation and wanted to leave the rest for this book because this philosophy of **Kintsukuroi** changed my life.

The Japanese potter usually makes the pots by hand with flexible clay. He shapes to pots then basically bakes them. Afterwards, they are left to dry and then you can shelf the beautiful work of art. Unfortunately, the pots are not indestructible and some crack/break over time. Now, some people would consider trying to fix it because they can still appreciate it even with a few cracks and obvious repairs and believe that they can elevate it to a whole new level of appreciation. While others would just throw it away because they fail to see the beauty after it has been broken.

Kintsukuroi means that instead of the damage weakening the pot's beauty, the new version actually raised appreciation higher than it was before. The pot had become more beautiful after being broken. A more prominent life for the pot began the moment it was broken. The people who choose to repair the pots do not mind having the obvious repairs incorporated into the aesthetic of the restored version. Doesn't having the obvious repairs incorporated into the beauty of the restored version of yourself seems more artistically "better than new"?

My take on it is this: Repair yourself with gold. When you decide to "work on yourself" it's so much less about the person who hurt you

45

and way way way more about your focus and effort to rediscover yourself and fill your voids with quality things and people. Remember: **The best thing that could come out of a broken heart is a better version of you.**

I believe that we should put effort every day creating new routines that are going to help us progress and reach our goals - Repairing the cracks with gold. Adding dope shit to your life. New shit. New dress code. New car. New place. New job. New everything... but why? Because you do not want to be that damaged person anymore. The new and positive things in your life reflect the newly increased quality of yourself.

You become more beautiful after being hurt when you add valuable things to fill the voids and stop calling yourself "damaged." How about saying that you are "recovering", "healing", or "working on yourself." Positive self-talk. Too many people accept being called "damaged"; feeling sorry for themselves and focusing on their mistakes and bullshit they've been through. But you have to get out of that funk: you do not belong there. You may have taken a few beatings to the heart but it still works and didn't kill you. Do yourself a favor... stop calling yourself broken or damaged. Try focusing more on improving. Block your ex and chill.

We are progressing, transforming, work in progress. We are in constant states of change. Our pain doesn't have to define our current version of ourselves, but can lead us to where we are going, and who we are becoming: The love of our lives. That's why you're not damaged. You're not broken. Your feelings are just hurt and the memories are very uncomfortable. You just need some motivation, positive self-talk and an understanding that we can become healed and made beautiful. I wouldn't trade the pain and experience I've gained throughout my life for anything because without them, I wouldn't know love, elegance or healing. It is what makes my life beautiful. **Kintsukuroi** is a reminder that all those cracks and breaks in our lives are what makes us beautiful.

Every day, be grateful for who you are.

Every day, forgive yourself.

Every day, treat yourself.

Every day, challenge yourself, do one thing that scares you, but also serves you well.

"Outside looking in."

I think it is easier to love someone than it is to love ourselves because it isn't the same kind of love. Loving someone else is objectively easy if we don't know very much about them, because we tend to fill in the missing pieces with our fantasies of who they are.

Loving ourselves is different. We know the bad things about ourselves. We know our own internal chaos. We are aware of the many times we have done things that were less than moral.

But, when we look at others, we see only what we want to see. "Outside looking in."

It's easy to see the beauty in another person. It's just as easy to see the guilt and self-loathing within ourselves.

This is why few people are willing to take an honest look at themselves.

It's sometimes easier to "love" others because we seldom really know who they are. At least not initially and sometimes not ever. Even when we do know, it's often easier to forgive others (for things that don't involve us) than it is to forgive ourselves.

Removing The Bullshit

We are often afraid of losing someone who we don't fully have. But why? Well, most times it is because we think that it hurts more to be without that person than it does to be with that person. See, we know what to expect when we are with them: lying, cheating, trying to forgive, great sex... blah, blah, blah and a few "good moments" that seems to last forever from the perspective of the heart. But, we don't REMEMBER much about how great life for ourselves used to be when we didn't have them because we've invested so much in THEM.

We become the product of their lies and disrespect. We are the sum of what they think of us. We are the total of how they make us feel and how we changed ourselves to please them. We forget how to function without them because we never thought that we would ever have to again. We forget who we used to be before them. We don't remember who we were and if we did, do we really want to go back to the version of ourselves that was so willing to give up everything for someone so undeserving? Hell no! We want to be better. The issue is that we want them to be better as well... for US. But what if we choose to dedicate ourselves to seeing what letting THEM go and lost-love could teach us?

What I'm not going to give you is a bunch of high five

ass answers to make everything well, but what I will give you is a little lane to ride towards recovery that worked for me. Regardless of how long you and your ex were together, it will feel strange to cut off all communication aka remove the bullshit. But that's actually the whole point! Letting that shit go so that you can grow.

Even if your ex has told you that they still want to "be friends" (most often its Bullshit) you still need to leave them alone for a while. Their presence will distract you, the sex will confuse you, the cooked meals and Netflix movie selection will sidetrack you. When it's time to move on (meaning you've made up your mind to move on), the presence of your ex needs to be flushed out (Like shit). How the hell are you going to get over someone who is in your damn face with a hand down your pants every day, questioning you about that other person who has been getting your attention? How the hell are you going to take care of your own business if you are still stalking the old bae's business all over social media? Just because your ex sticks around all jealous and shit doesn't mean they want you. They sometimes just don't want you to go anywhere so you can be their lay-a-way booty call. You KNOW this.

Aside from some parenting situations or life-threatening scenarios where you HAVE to contact your ex, you should do everything you can during the "no communication" phase to avoid speaking to them at all other than about the kids, bills etc.

The Single People's Club

What does it mean to be single?

- only one; not one of several.
- an individual person or thing rather than part of a pair or a group.
- unmarried or not involved in a stable sexual relationship. You are legally single if you are not legally married. You are socially single if you are not in a romantic relationship that other people regard as serious. You are personally single if you think of yourself as single and not in a serious relationship.

I know a lot of people consider anyone who is not married to be single. But, not everyone wants to be married. My guess is these same people would say a "seriously exclusive relationship" is NOT a "commitment" unless the couple is married. If "exclusive" doesn't mean commitment then they're single, according to those people. They believe that the highest level of commitment that tells the world a person has given up the single life for good is marriage, but I think that the highest level of commitment that tells the world a person has given up the single life for good is the long term PROOF. Meaning, regardless of being married or not, if you say that you are all for someone, you prove it for the rest of your life. Of course some will say, "you might as

51

well be married," but like I said, not everyone wants to be married and they have their reasons.

I personally believe that not everyone wants to be married, but some people still value "commitment". To me, single means one. If you are in a relationship, then there are 2 people committed. If you are dating a person exclusively and another person comes along and asks you on a date, you should not date them if you say you are in a committed relationship. I consider single to be a person who is not in a COMMITTED relationship. If you are dating around or not dating at all then you are single.

Discrimination Against Singles

We live in a society where people feel that you must have a partner with whom you can live happily ever after. However, I'm convinced SOME people in long-term relationships are secretly miserable. Sure, it's nice to have someone official to Netflix and Chill with, but relationships can be unpleasantly problematic.

If you are single right now, whatever the reason, you can believe that your life right now still has special value. Don't let bitter ass people in committed relationships make you feel like you're a nobody just because you don't have someone. Being single isn't a death sentence. There are plenty of happy single people in this world who have already realized that working on themselves always beats being thirsty as hell for a relationship. Don't forget that there are a lot of people who are in relationships who wish they weren't.

Besides, if you don't love yourself, a relationship with someone else isn't going to solve the problem or truly fulfil you anyways. In that case, your ass needs to be single to work on yourself instead of letting society pressure you into fuck buddy Situationships and into being in a relationship that you're not ready for. We can't allow this institutionalized prejudice about being single drive us to be in relationships with the "wrong" person for the wrong reasons: loneliness, sex and attention.

For women in particular, it seems as though Society pressures them into relationships the most. When they meet a guy, and start hanging around him for a few months, they race to pushing for a relationship title and seeing him in the future. One reason why they seem to do that is because Society will say that they are being "hoes" for wasting their time entertaining a single guy for so long. It's like they pressure her as if she must be in a relationship in order to hang around a man and be respected.

I just want you to know that the relationship status isn't the only thing that defines who we are. Most single people have discovered that being single means so much more than not having a relationship partner, it's about having a great relationship with "self" regardless of whether or not you have a partner.

Benefits of Being Single

We finally have the time to be single, to go out whenever we want without someone clocking our time. As single people, we have the opportunity to enjoy the independence and freedom that our "committed" friends often wish they had. We finally have all of the free time in the world and no one holding us down or messing with our heads. We finally have some "me" time. This is the time to reconnect with ourselves, and a time where we can motivate ourselves.

This is the time of reflection. This is the time of acceptance and letting go. When we are single, we start paying more attention to ourselves and how we look and what we want in life. Also, it is not easy to make new friends while in a relationship because we spend so much time together and some people grow to be excessively jealous of your social interactions. Now, while single, you don't have to ditch your girls on singles night at the dance club or you don't have to ditch your boys and finally hit the strip club.

The best part about it is that after healing, we get to start over with SOMEONE NEW.

helps open our eyes to how many others love us.

Often times, we get so caught up in a relationship that we forget that love isn't just for a romantic partner. After a break up, friends and family are on our sides. Not only do we feel more love from them, but stronger connections are created as well. Not all misery wants company, so when our single homegirls or homies tell us to "cut that bullshit off", it's not because they want us to be single with them, or because they are hating on us, they just don't want our asses to keep looking and feeling stupid for staying in a fake happy relationship.

helps us learn to be alone without feeling lonely.

They say that the simple answer to loneliness is surrounding ourselves with other people, but that's not always an option—or something that we want. When we are feeling lonely, it is because something has activated a memory of that feeling, not because we are actually alone. We can be out with friends and because something has reminded us of that lonely feeling, we end up feeling lonely in a crowd.

Lonely Reminders

Feeling lonely can come from the memories of the past and hope for the future, but there's usually something in the present that jogs your memory. You can counter the effect of some reminders by removing them. Maybe you put the photos and old love notes away in the back of the closet or just throw them away so that you don't randomly see them. Maybe it's about time you unfollow them from social media. Or maybe it's time to ditch some of the sentimental items. Delete songs that make you sad and add songs that will put you in the mood that you WANT to be in. Have something to go to for when you feel loneliness creeping up on you. Whatever it is that can shift the thoughts in your mind, always have it ready.

Or, try to be more creative with your alone time. Creative people actually crave alone time because it gives them freedom and space to express themselves how THEY want to which results in feeling refreshed mentally. To experience the beauty of solitude, you can write, draw, read, go to school, paint or get a new job.

But I avoid:

Drinking by myself.

Having sex with random people just because.

Watching Netflix and browsing social media so much that it becomes a substitute for socializing.

Or doing things JUST to repress the memories. If you're going to do something, at least let it be something productive and something that you actually like doing.

I think It is okay not
to be COMPLETELY
ready for everything
I claim I deserve. If
I can admit that, then
I already know it's
better to be honest and
patient with myself
and grow, than to try and
rush things just
because I have a few
lonely nights. I don't
want to ruin the potential
of what could be
good for me later down
the road, by trying
to jump into something too
soon. I just want
to make sure it's right and
take time to appreciate it.

Horacio Jones

I AM THE LOVE OF MY LIFE

You realize that "the one" is YOU.

I found myself trying to be what I thought would be most accepted. I would always go through the trouble of trying to impress others and prove my worth, to no avail. I'd transform myself to a false persona and I had failed to realize that my authentic self was more than enough. Breaking up and removing the bullshit was definitely a wake-up call. I believe that waking up to who you are requires letting go of who you imagined yourself to be with someone and accepting who you are as an individual without them.

Even though the love may not have lasted, you learned more about your own worth. You learn that you are good enough because you let that person go who hurt you and chose to move forward with your life. You understood that you were worth more than the way you were treated. You learned to move on. You've sat down and drowned in yourself and truly known what it means to be YOU.

Quickly, you discovered that many of the things you thought you wanted in a partner aren't what you really needed. The loss forces you to face new challenges and hold your head up, even when you don't really feel like it. Though it might be hard to see at first, the broken heart actually helps free you up for the right person.

It's really
over once
my heart
rejects you

Horacio Jones

I AM THE LOVE OF MY LIFE

Willing to get hurt again

Being single is the time period
where we review the relationships
and Situationships we've been in.
Being single is where we forgive
who hurt us, ... and forgive
ourselves for staying so long. Being
single is about finding peace with
ourselves, rediscovering ourselves,
and loving ourselves. After that,
it's time to test what we've learned
while being single and date again.
The lessons of our pasts have
prepared us for dating as the new
version of ourselves. Of course we're
not going to feel ready because we
haven't dated as this new version yet.
But, there is no such thing as a sure
thing in dating/mingling. It's always a
gamble. It's always a risk. Take it.

It's a necessary risk if we want to build
something with someone other than
ourselves. And if we want to stay single,
there's nothing wrong with that. Open up and
go on a date this week. Just try it. The date can
be simple, not very long, dinner, talk, back
home to review how it felt to be out as the
new version of you in the presence of a new
love interest. If you feel the need to utilize
Netflix and chill, why not cook together, set a
dinner table, even dress-up, and actually have
deep conversations, then watch Netflix?

I like being alone.
I have control over
my own space.
Therefore,
in order to win me
over, your presence
has to be better than
my solitude. You're
not competing with
another person, you
are competing with
my comfort zone

Horacio Jones

Solitude

I am not sure when, but somewhere down the line being single became the same as feeling lonely. I get it, solitude and Loneliness appears to be very similar on the outside. However, they are both tremendously different experiences. While solitude is chosen, loneliness is forced by our feelings. Loving solitude is the desire to be in our own presence and enjoy our own company. Loneliness is a feeling of worthlessness and isolation, and that someone or something is missing. When you enjoy your solitude, you will work to develop the creative fundamentals of expressing yourself. It will be called Art, meditation, the universe, religion and Science, and you will not be *lonely*.

Ever.

My imagination and curiosity are enough to occupy my mind. My solitude is my favorite thing. In the silent moments of solitude, I think about love, about myself and the world around me and discover who I am, what I truly love and what I want out of life.

I naturally feel like going places alone and enjoying the scene, thinking and maybe write in my Instagram journal. I usually feel extremely relaxed and peaceful. It's a wonderful feeling and a very healthy thing, I believe.

I think that being an introvert makes it easier to be single. Yeah, I think of having a woman sometimes and sex and all that, but it doesn't drive me crazy or torment me when I don't have those things or people around me. I'm currently good with or without someone next to me.

I'm learning to step out of my zone but I just don't feel the same satisfaction when I'm out with people a lot. I love being out, but on my own.

Most People Are Annoying.

I don't enjoy small talk and I actually suck at it. I can hardly hold a pointless conversation for more than a few seconds. Even with texts. And it annoys me that I have to make those conversations just because people will think I'm a jerk for not speaking or for exiting conversations quickly.

In solitude, you are free to do whatever you want. There isn't anyone to judge you. No one will make fun of you, or bother you.

A lot of people fake most of their personality just to be liked/appreciated more. They lie about their taste in music, the stuff they enjoy, the stuff they hate just to appear likeable. But as you spend more time with them, you realize the truth and its irritating.

I don't get why most people are scared of being alone. I love it. Spending time with yourself in tranquility, reflecting on things is as crucial to our growth as is happiness and contentment around groups of people. Solitude is underrated and nowadays people would do anything to avoid being lonely because being alone is often associated with depression, when really it should be symbolic for self-love and appreciation for your own energy/light.

What is it like to be an introvert?

It's like throwing parties where you are the
only person attending and having the
time of your life every time.

It's like going to a party with 100 people and
thinking, "this shit would be so lit if
at least 96 people left."

We have rich inner worlds full of imagination.

Myth About Introverts

Introverts don't like to talk.
Get an introvert talking about
something they are interested in,
and they won't shut up for days.

Introverts are shy.
Not always true. What they
need is a different reason to
interact. If you want to
talk to me, just start talking.

Introverts don't like people.
Actually, we intensely value
the few friends and close
family members we have.

Introverts don't like going out in public.

We just don't like to go out in
public FOR A LONG TIME.

Introverts always want to be alone.
Actually, we crave authentic and
sincere connections with FEW
PEOPLE.

Introverts are weird.
False. We just don't follow
the crowds and trends.

*Introverts don't know how to relax and have
fun.*
False. We rather relax at home or in
nature, not in busy public places.

Introverts secretly want to be Extroverts.
Introverts actually like being introverts;
it is our natural temperament.

Don't Run Back

Ok, let's be completely realistic now. Removing someone from your life is one of those easier said than done type of things. In my experience, time is your friend, but not the cure. Meeting new people and starting new hobbies are ingredients but not the cure. The cure is not distracting yourself... you heal when you deal.

I think that the reality for most of us who have trouble "moving on" is that we actually do not WANT to. Sometimes, even when we "want" to, our subconscious mind has not yet let go because we try to ignore the pain, hoping it would just go away on its own. And the next thing we know, we are right back stressing over our exes while lying in their beds after **hypnosis-sex.** WHY is it that the old flame always looks more appealing after we leave? Why can't we just get over them and move on?

Most times we just sit there expecting that all we have to do is give it time, start a distracting routine, hurry to date new people or find new hobbies but we still end up feeling lonely because those things don't address the bigger issues... that we are afraid to actually deal with the break up. We try to run from the pain by suppressing it and hiding it behind fake happy Instagram pictures. We don't realize this but fear drives us backwards... to the past, to our exes, to what we already know doesn't work.

The truth is that we have to deal so that we can heal and build enough strength to not allow the pain and loneliness to drive us right back. We must find both the positive and negative aspects of the broken relationship and turn them both into positive self-empowering reasons to accept that the purpose of the relationship has been served and lessons have been learned so that the fear of being alone and missing someone doesn't drive us back to those who do not deserve us.

Lonely and Bored

Let's take a deeper look into loneliness because this may be the number one thing that drives us to "run back." When we associate feeling lonely with missing someone, we are heading in the wrong direction; "backwards". Most times we aren't necessarily missing *them*, we are likely grief-stricken by the end of the life that was supposed to be built with them and either horny or bored. Life teaches us that giving in to loneliness keeps us stuck in the cycle of running back to our old relationships or Situationships.

Lonely or Alone?

Are you alone or are you lonely? Like I mentioned, I enjoy being alone most of the time, but I do have feelings of loneliness at times. When I am feeling lonely, its due to not liking being alone. It has led me to believe that loneliness is a disease and isn't measurable by the amount of other bodies around you. It is measured by what you personally feel whether you're alone or in a crowd. It is a negative emotion and a negative state of mind where you are longing for another person. The result of loneliness is sadness.

A *lonely* person is not usually a happy person. Loneliness is when you are unhappy because you are alone or because you have no friends, committed relationship partner or booty calls. When you're lonely, you're always looking elsewhere for fulfillment. You're not content with having no one around you. It is when you are yearning for someone that you do not have anymore, or maybe never fully had. You can even feel lonely when you have someone there physically but not emotionally.

Being *alone* on the other hand, simply means that it's just you and no one else. It doesn't mean that you don't have anyone else, it just means that you don't need them or have them around and that you are content with your own solitude. When you are alone, you can still feel whole and not lonely. You can be happy even when alone because your contentment comes from inside of you. Your self-worth is not dependent upon any external people or things. Being alone frees you from distraction if you're working on things that requires focus. Sometimes it helps to have no one around when you're trying to get shit done efficiently.

My belief is that before we can jump into another relationship, whether it be a friend with benefits

Situationship or a real committed one on one relationship, we should first learn the joy of being by our damn selves for once. If you search for someone or something to fill the void of your loneliness, you will find the exact same thing: Another person who is lonely as hell and looking only for what's initially convenient or to fill a void and probably "not looking for anything serious." So, if you don't like being alone and feel lonely, find people with similar interests to vibe with. Yes, that means you may have to get off your ass and step out of your comfort zone a bit and MAKE time for other humans that you would WANT around you and not continue to allow the same "nothing serious" type people try to convert you into their dating style: Situationships.

How To Be Happy And Alone

You can be happy while being "*alone*" by deciding to use loneliness as fuel to be more productive, find better people to connect with and making sure that the cold, lonely and horny nights don't get to you. Even if you hate your loneliness, know that sometimes all you can do is suck it up and move the fuck on. Sometimes you have no choice, so you should rather get active than being bitter about it.

Lessons I've learned while being alone

1. Spending time alone teaches you life lessons.
2. Being alone increases creativity.
3. Even when I really want a relationship with

someone who loves me, I know that I do not rely solely on that relationship to function.
4. Spending time alone removes distractions.
5. No matter the circumstances, I can still be ok.
6. You become more productive.
7. Happiness comes from within.
8. I can create my own happiness.
9. Being alone can be healthy.
10. You will stop looking for approval from others.

Sexually Frustrated And Bored

Sometimes, you just miss the sex, not the certain *person*. Missing someone based on boredom and being thirsty for sex are really good reasons to stay away. We call it *Sexual frustration*. Sexual frustration means you're horny and you haven't gotten any sex to relieve the sexual tension and you don't have anything else to do that would keep your mind off of sex. To be sexually frustrated means that a person is irritated because they are not receiving a gratifying sexual release as often as they would like. And since they don't want to sleep around and the sex was really good with an ex, they miss that comfortable sex situation, not really the specific person. They choose to recycle exes.

This is where we get really creative in convincing ourselves that it is okay to step back in just a little. We want to spend one night. Send one text. Make one call. But, then it turns into more random nights, multiple long "I miss you" texts, and hours on the phone. You'll be feeling like it's all going good, so why back off? You miss the calm periods, right? It's all calm because there is no pressure or commitment. There are no rules, you're just "talking." We convince ourselves that its harmful and we won't let the feelings get the best of us again. It's all the proof that when we said we were ready to move on we were lying to ourselves.

It isn't okay but we love to convince ourselves that it is. Let's face it, you can't be a little involved with an ex; it's all or nothing. When you are just a little involved, you're still going to think about them a lot. You will think of how things used to be. If only. A little involvement will make a lot of involvement seem appealing if that little involvement is peaceful. And those thoughts of peace make sense because maybe you can only tolerate that person just a little bit. But what happens when you start to spend more days, minutes, hours, chill sessions, sex sessions? Suddenly, that little involvement becomes a big involvement. Now you're damn near past half way back together (not fully because you agreed to the "let's be friends again first" phrase) and you start to see all of the reasons why you left in the first place: you can't trust or stand them.

Side Note

***Don't fall victim to the "let's work on being friends again first," line that people use to keep you on lay away. What the fuck is "let's work on being friends first" with someone you've been in a relationship with for years

already? Do you know what's going to happen? You're going to "build" that friendship, they are going to get comfortable, and have sex... next thing you know, there's no relationship, you settled for less but you're acting like it is a real relationship until they remind you "we are not together." You spent all of that time "building a friendship" and proving your worth, knowing damn well you don't want to be "friends." You want to be together in a romantic relationship. But you spend all of that time investing in what you don't want, just to realized that you got played by your own horniness, loneliness, boredom and ex out of what you do want.

I AM THE LOVE OF MY LIFE

Missing Someone

Sometimes people leave your life out of nowhere and all that's left are the memories. Sometimes you might not care at first, and then when their absence fully sinks in, it eats you alive. At first, your mind will try to forget the memory of their existence. Then, it will look for ways to distract you from the memories that are too hard to forget. It gets hard to figure out if you miss the person or just feeling lonely.

When we miss someone, we have an intense urge to call that specific person, text that specific person and can't get them out of our minds. When you miss the person, you miss very specific things about them as well. You miss their voice or the way they'd imessage you at exactly 8:14 in the morning. You even miss the things you swore you never would. Like their taste in trap music. Or how frustrated you'd get at them when they'd get petty with you because you posted on Instagram before texting them back. You'll miss how well you knew them. You miss the things about them that drove you crazy. Like how after you'd write them a text message, they'd write back only one word. How you could predict when you'll receive a call or visit from them. And even now you'd do just about anything to see their name pop up on your phone. The biggest indicator is when you want someone around you, and the only person you can think of is that specific person. No matter how many times you try to hang out with other people, you want THAT specific person to be around you. But when you just miss not being alone, you only miss generally having a body there.

Healthy Selfishness

Society teaches that selfishness is bad, so a generation of "I need to over prove my worth and give, give, give just to get someone to want me" is the result. And we all know that those type of people often get taken advantage of. Realistically it's necessary to have a balance of selflessness and selfishness if you want to be happy, even if you have been taught that it's bad to be selfish.

Think about this: Everything that you do every day that contributes to your own survival or pleasure is an act of selfishness. We are all selfish to some degree. But, healthy selfishness is a process of managing those desires and needs. Meaning, there are limits.

If we do not focus on ourselves and take care of our own needs, we become weak, needy and drain life from those around us. To be focused on ourselves in a healthy way is to take responsibility and taking care of ourselves is part of living a mindful life. If this is called selfishness than this form of selfishness is healthy because it reminds us of our responsibility to take care of our own shit first rather than burden others to take care of our needs.

When we truly take care of ourselves without expectations from others, we get to BE HAPPY NOW, and we know we are getting our needs met because we are personally meeting them. Therefore, selfishness is actually a way of taking care of yourself. So, the next time you begin to wonder if you're being selfish, ask yourself if you're taking care of yourself or not.

the difference between selfishness and self-love: If you are selfish, you always put yourself ahead others. Selfishness means that you make sure your needs are met first, always. Self-love means that you make sure your needs are not always met last; you put others before you, but not always.

Love Languages

"I believe that relationships will last
longer if both people would learn
each other's love language. If you can
understand how someone shows their
love, and accept that their way
will differ from yours, you can actually
grow closer together through that
understanding. Just because they
show love differently than you show
it doesn't mean that they do not love you"

Your definition of love is your own. NEVER judge any other person's love by your definition of love because they might have a different definition and different way of showing it. If you want to find out whether a person really loves you or not, just ask them what is their definition of love and then silently observe their actions to see if those actions fit their definition. If they are not able to give their own definition of love, then it is likely (but not certain) that they are only infatuated. If their actions do not match their definition, look harder. And if it still does not match, they are being inconsistent with what they have defined as THEIR love.

We tend to misinterpret others' actions according to our definition instead of theirs. Having taken that caution, if it still doesn't match, then you need to learn about their love language more or they need to explain and demonstrate it better. I think that we often expect people to love us damn near exactly like we love them, and when they don't reciprocate what we put in, we complain about it or say that they just do not love us back. That's not fair, to try to make people love like we do.

Is Love Really Blind?

No, it's just that when we
are in love, we simply perceive
things differently. Love sees
you for who you really are,
and enhances your ability to
ignore what you don't like
about people and focus more
on what you do like about them.
You SEE the red flags but you
also see their potential. Love
helps you see the "brighter side"

When we are in love, we perceive things differently. People who have "fallen out of love" phrase it as "love is blind" because they looked back on the relationship and realized all of the signs they "didn't see", but in fact it's the complete opposite. When you are in love, you end up accepting the other person along with their flaws, some bad habits and mistakes because you can either tolerate it or SEE the potential of working on those things during the relationship. You are aware of these things. You SEE them.

But sometimes things don't work out because of those things that you THOUGHT you could tolerate or "fix." When it's all over and your feelings fade, you remember all of those flaws and SEE even clearer just how annoying they were but at the time, you were ignoring the signs because there was a greater force helping you SEE the brighter side: LOVE. Love helps you SEE the BEST in people, and deal with the worst.

Be happy for your exes who find happiness even when they hurt you in the past and still managed to move on before you. But also do not allow your ex moving on make you feel like you are "not enough" or like you need to rush to find someone else for you.

Working On Myself

We should only put our love lives on hold if we are trying to heal emotionally. But if we are working on ourselves by going to school, work etc. Then yeah, we could make room in our lives for dating. However, I think that if we know we're completely hurt, we should not be involving anyone else in our bullshit until we get a grip.

Logically speaking, it is possible to work on yourself while working on the relationship if you can find a healthy balance. When I'm working on myself emotionally, closure from a past relationship etc... I make no plans to date until the work is minimized (work on self is never "100% done"). I will be working on myself for the rest of my life. I'll never be complete or finished because there will always be something new to add and more to work on. So, at what part of the "working on myself" stage should you date again? I'm not waiting until I'm "finished" to date. And I actually don't want a "finished" lover. I want to be able to build together.

Working on yourself

So when someone says, "I have to work on myself first," it is like saying "I have to focus on JUST me. Not US. But we may be able to work on something after I'm more content with just me." That's ok. Nothing wrong with that. But what I have a problem with is when you feel like you have to focus on just you and you purposely try to string someone along while you settle down with only giving half the effort.

It's not always intentional, sometimes you truly may feel as though you can work on yourself and a relationship with someone else at the same time. Other times, you feel like you

81

have to only focus on yourself, and opt out of dating for a while. But I can't stand "sometimey" people. Sometimes they want you, sometimes they don't. Sometimes they can work on a relationship, sometimes they can only work on themselves.

Look, if you have to work on yourself only, go do that if you feel like you have to do that on your own. But no one wants to be halfway together with you. Keep in mind that they are also working on themselves and choosing to correspondingly work on a relationship with you too.

See, we will never stop working on ourselves. THATS what you don't get. Every day, you have to take care of **you**, you have to eat, clean, exercise and figure out your next move. So making someone wait until you're "together" is like making them wait forever. There's always more "pieces" to add to the self, so how will you ever be "done" ....

When are you ready to work on you **AND** A relationship with more than half of your heart? Overall, it depends on how much work you think you need to put into yourself that determines when you're ready to date again. Also, you have to find a person that is willing to be supportive and understanding. They have to know that at times, somethings are a priority above them because you are working on improving. It goes both ways.

Intuition

"Sometimes it's hard to hear your own voice"

Dear self,

Intuition is unconscious reasoning. As we learn things about people, we begin to recognize patterns. Good ones and bad ones. And when something isn't "adding up," or that significant other does something similar to something that someone else made a habit of doing, your intuition sends out an alert for your own good, but **sometimes** it's hard to hear your own voice.

Your "Gut feeling" is nothing more than your brain recognizing similar patterns from the past. It is the sum of your knowledge on a certain situation and has a tendency to be more accurate than decisions you spend a lot of time weighing the pros and cons for because you have been there and done that physically or mentally before. It either happened to you or to someone you know. Therefore, you should go with your "gut feeling" when you have a high level of relevant personal experience or experience through other people and you can't make any logical conclusion.

Are you intuitive or insecure?

Maybe you don't trust your intuition because you're waiting for the hard-core facts. So you stick it out as long as you can while searching for those facts. You might stalk their social media. You might check their call log and text messages. You might check their emails. It's because you feel something eating at you within, but you can't actually see the proof in physical form. So you investigate.

When hard core facts FINALLY slap you in the face, it hurts but also puts you at ease if you accept it as the truth and not start trying to switch over to prove that what you see is not real. But what if you never get those hardcore facts? Are you going to stick around while your intuition is eating you alive?

I get it... Breaking up with someone because of a "feeling" just doesn't feel like it's legit enough. The crazy thing is, the more you ignore your intuition, the more insecure you become. Your intuition is the universe telling you that something isn't right and to trust the signs. Insecurity is when you just don't feel like you're enough or worth it. When you're intuitive, you feel like you're worth it while also feeling like THEY are the problem, not you. When you're insecure, you feel like YOU are the problem.

I know you don't want to break up over a gut feeling (intuition) so you stay, waiting for the facts to confirm everything. The sad thing is that they'll call you CRAZY, Insecure, overthinking, "in your feelings," and exaggerate it all as long as you'll believe them. Then all of a sudden, you'll start thinking about all of the rash decisions you've been making based on these growing insecurities.... Really believing you're insecure.

The fear of accepting the truth can result in those gut feelings being pushed aside in favor of what may be perceived to be the 'easier' option. Never ignore the signals. If you follow your gut, you'll not only make decisions more quickly, but most of the time they'll be better, too.

I have come to this rule: If you **feel** the exact answer, (your mind is telling you, your body is telling you...) it is easy - choose **THAT** one. When your gut feeling is in line with your logic... If your intuition and your rational thinking are telling you the same thing, you probably have nothing to worry about. Choose what your body and mind is telling you.

When is following your gut a bad choice?

Think about the kind of track record your gut feeling has. Did you follow your feelings and later regretted it? Or did you ignore your intuition and wish you had listened? The past will let you know if your intuition is reliable.

"I Am In Love With You"
Vs. "I Have Love For You"

Both expressions are beautiful
in their proper perspectives.

Love, in its truest sense,
is something that you do
and not just something
that you feel.

"I have love for you" means I have it...
It's inside of me. But it's not lugging
me towards you to give it to you.

"I am in love with you" means that I
have a passionate desire to show you
and give you all of the love that I have
for you. I want YOU to have it.

When you say "I am in love with you",
this is moving love to its greatest stage:
deeper feelings that you want to actively
express to the other person - love becomes
an action. Whereas "I have love" only
requires thought, emotional recognition,
awareness of how much you care,
but not having a desire
for intimacy.

"I am in love with you" is acceptance and submission to the feeling, **"I have love for you"** states the complete control over the feeling. Which one would you desire? I am all yours or I am yours only when I'm feeling horny and drunk? The difference in these two phrases is how each one illustrates the kind of love. "I have love for you" might mean that the given love is a general feeling like they have for friends and family... people they care deeply about. The "I am in love with you" expression is very specific and specifies a deeper and greater volume of love.

There are times when you "have" or possess love for someone. I have always considered this to be love in its relaxing state. It accumulates from the experiences that you have with them, or from sincere care for them. When speaking of "having love" for a particular person, it could be appreciation for that person and the role they play in your life. It becomes "in love" when these feelings build up inside of you so much that you feel the need to show them on a different level: **intimacy.**

Timing

Dear self, is timing really *everything*?

The words time and timing are used commonly, but they reflect two very different meanings despite the element of time in them. We all know what time is, but some people get confuse between these two terms.

> *Time is the duration,*
> *"timing" is specific*
> *points in time.*

Timing is a gigantic part in relationship success. You can meet a good person, but if you meet at a "bad" time, it's not as likely to work. Almost everyone who has ever fallen for someone else has probably been the victim of shitty timing. The truth is, it sucks until you finally meet a good person at a good time and things naturally fall into place. Of course, it still takes effort and everything else, like compatibility and chemistry.

They say timing is just another excuse we use when we're not up for the mission of building a relationship. Many say that if they are experiencing difficult circumstances in their lives, they cannot commit to someone else. That's true for some of us because you should never put someone else's happiness above your own.

**You should never drag someone else
through your mud if you know you
cannot help them out and you have
to make sure your own shit is taken
care of before you take care of
someone else's.**

We have to take care of our disasters in life. But do we
have to go through those difficult *times* alone? If you are
in a *time* in your life where bringing someone else along
for the ride will only do more damage than good, then
yeah, get your shit straight on your own first, then involve
them later. But if someone who loves you can assist you
and is strong enough to get through it all with you, why
not let them? If you're at a low point in your life but you
have someone that, under better circumstances, would
be with you in a relationship, they can still be in your life.
They can still be someone who doesn't take you off of
your path to self-love. Sometimes, the time that you
meet them is at a time where you don't feel good about
adjusting your life to fit them in. That is ok.

I'll be the first to admit that I can spend months alone
if I'm too scared, too hurt or just not ready to put myself
back out there. That's when I'm seriously rejecting even
the best type of people for me because I don't want to
hurt them by randomly falling back after feeling like the
connection was overwhelming. I could be going through a
lot at a certain point in life when someone amazing
comes along, but I don't feel like the *timing* is right.
Maybe I don't feel ready to invest. Or I won't give the

connection enough time to grow. I'd tell them that I didn't have enough *time* but it was actually due to fear, not really the *timing*. I think we sometimes use "bad timing" as a cop out to justify our unwillingness to step up and make decisions. We sometimes miss the best thing that could probably happen to us, but blame it on bad *timing* because we are lazy daters or because we are too scared.

Time and *time* again, we've all had to face that raw realization that if he or she really cared as much as we did, they would have moved mountains to make things happen. The same thing for us. If we really cared, no matter what *time* it is, we'd put effort to make ourselves ready to be loved and give love.

"Bad Timing" can definitely be a convenient excuse, but in a lot of cases it is the real reason. If two people really want to be together, they will both put in effort to try to make it work. It's possible that after trying, one or both may feel like it's not worth the effort, but there has to be at least an honest attempt. Basically, I can only think of a handful of circumstances where *timing* is a real, genuine reason to end a relationship that both people are honestly in to.

Bad Times in Your Life to Start a Relationship

1. When you are just getting out of a relationship: If you are feeling depressed, lonely and helpless, and you just want to cry on somebody's shoulder, then you need a good friend, not a relationship.
2. When being in a relationship sounds easier than being alone. If you need someone, that means you are dependent, and this will

make any relationship awkward.
3.   When traveling alone constantly.
4.   Just because you feel obligated.

The truth is, there is never a perfect time to begin a relationship. The stability of one relies on the balance of mental, physical and emotional strength and maturity of both people. However, waiting for one person to be completely content at the same exact time as you are concurrently is usually seen as a "waste of time." Expecting two people to be ready simultaneously is often unrealistic. One person will be ready before the other and sometimes the other person makes themselves ready, or they choose to "not be ready for a relationship" ... with YOU. For a relationship to function healthily you don't always need perfect conditions, timing or for both of you to be at the same level of readiness; what you do need is to be open, honest and familiar with each other. What you need is understanding of each other's love languages and communication. What you need is both people to be willing to commit and build during whatever "**timing.**"

I am a hopeless romantic, and I truly believe that relationships can flourish under less than ideal circumstances. What matters most in these situations is that both people are fully aware of the odds that are against them. What matters is having someone who will understand your challenge to commit at that specific **time**, and they will still be there for you. What matters is that both of you are still willing to take the risk and

"time" for forming a relationship.

You cannot invest in me if you're not investing in yourself. I find it so heartbreaking to deal with someone who makes me their everything but refuses to make themselves anything. I don't want to be the only one loving you in the relationship

Horacio Jones

Dear busy people,

One of your biggest fears is that you think the next person is going to waste your time. You've spent time learning more about yourself and loving yourself, and you don't want to fuck up the progress by making yourself available to someone and have them take it all for granted. Nonetheless deep down inside, you really want a relationship... but keep telling people that you are too busy.

How about you try to adjust your time according to your priorities? Real priorities. Significant ones. "Busy watching Netflix" isn't significant. Busy taking a nap isn't significant. "Chilling" isn't busyness.

Maybe you are in a situation where you cannot afford to spend less time at work, school etc.

Maybe you need to work multiple jobs, you have kids and taking care of a parent, to put food on the table, for example. In that case, a relationship is most likely not going to happen right now, unless you MAKE TIME for it.

If a free and fun relationship is what you want, maybe it's time to work on changing your lifestyle so it can happen someday. You become a very annoying person when you claim to be so busy, yet you're still out trying to halfway date people, while they want to fully date you.

There is a difference between being busy with

important things and knocking the person in your life further and further down your priority list. If you feel like you're waiting for someone to spend significant time with you more than you're actually spending time with them, it's time to step back and take another look at where your relationship is going. People make time for who they want to make time for. If they are too busy to nurture a relationship, why the fuck are they in one?

Busyness Is A Choice

Dear self,

Busyness makes us feel like we are important. It keeps us from feeling empty because we fill our time with things that are either significant, mandatory or interesting and entertaining. Busyness is a sign that you are in demand and in control. When we feel busy, we feel like we're winning at life— like we're doing something right and maximizing our productivity. When we are able to tell people that we are **"too busy"** to do this or that thing, it makes us feel significant while being sought-after.

But, have you noticed that it isn't normally the people pulling multiple shifts at work or traveling between cities to two jobs and to school who tell you how busy they are; those people are more tired than busy. They choose to be busy. They're busy because of their own drive and ambition. They feel anxious and guilty when they aren't handling their priorities. They don't want to leave things undone so they choose to make time to take care of what is important.

The funny thing is damn near everyone else I know says that they are busy. They are not working on anything that they have to do. The truth is, the people who are doing all of that complaining about being busy often use it as an excuse for why they can't see you or date you. They aren't really busy because things are completely mandatory, they choose things to do other than seeing you, and they call that being "busy".

I AM THE LOVE OF MY LIFE

Realize that being busy is a choice. It is a decision we make. We are never forced into a lifestyle of busyness. Your life will become less busy when you realize that most of your daily activities are determined by you. We have a choice in what we spend our time doing. We don't have to live busy lives. I hate saying that I am busy. "I'm too busy" is a slap in the face to whomever you're saying it to. You might as well tell the person, "Everything else in my life, even non-significant things, are exponentially more important and worth more of my time than you."

I AM THE LOVE OF MY LIFE

I am not busy. I have plenty of **"leisure time"**, I've just become accustomed to multi-tasking during my downtime—browsing social media while I watch Netflix, checking emails while I'm out to dinner, texting and snap chatting while I'm working out. I'm doing so many different kinds of **none important** things throughout the day that they all blend into important things and the day has no sense of distinct **"free time."**

Those unimportant things that I do concurrently with important things actually slows down my productivity and extends the duration of those important things. What I could have done in 2 hours lasted 4 hours because I stopped to post on Instagram, I facetimed bae, I looked for Yeezy Boost 350 on sale online, I called my ex, I snap chatted my food before and after and I took a nap because I felt **"tired"** and too busy. Sometimes, I can become so busy with **non-significant** things mixed with significant ones that I reach a tipping point where things fall apart because I can no longer endure the weight of so many commitments. Once I get to that point, it becomes obvious that I'm busy by choice.

Too Busy For A Relationship

You are working. You are going to school. You pride yourself on being independent and owning everything. Those things are most important to you. But, the reason why you can't find time for a good relationship is because you won't make time for it. Maybe you only make a small amount of time. The issue with that is that people who are seriously dating want more than the bare minimum or what's just convenient for you. They want a little bit more than you are willing to give. The time that you do set aside for dating actually attracts a certain type of date.

Here is a scenario: you want sex and some attention but you don't want to make a whole bunch of adjustments in your life to fit someone else in fully, you just want a little bit of sex here and there to keep the sexual frustration away and you want some attention every now and then so you won't feel too lonely. The type of person who makes *"I don't want anything serious"* sound worth it comes along and you connect with them because "you don't want anything serious either...."

Now, if you're always busy, you will feel like you don't have time for a relationship, BUT you'll make some time for this other person because they aren't pressuring you to commit to them full time. So, this means that what's convenient for you is also convenient for them. This works out for a while UNTIL you catch stronger feelings (but you thought you could control that smh) and want more than sex; more than attention. You want a real relationship. However, the other person doesn't. They like how things are arranged now and all they wanted from you was your *convenient time*, not your full time. All of a sudden, you feel busier because you're doing more than what you had planned on doing for them, since you want them fully *now*. If you are too busy for a relationship, you should also be too busy to handle a loyal booty call arrangement that's disguised as a relationship. Don't play yourself.

Emotion Control

*Welcome to the generation of "don't
catch feelings... I can control my
emotions."*

People who can **"control their emotions"** scare me. They supposedly *can't* fall in love. They "block" their real feelings, so they say, and it infers that they have total control over their emotions. They decide who to love and when they love them. According to them, they don't "catch feelings", they choose them, but become the main ones overwhelmed by emotions after having sex with you because they simply didn't know that they would end up liking you *THAT* much. I guess they lose control?

I don't think we can actually "hide feelings" or "hold feelings back." I've never controlled my feelings, only my actions. Maybe that's what people mean; they don't want to actively show you how they feel for whatever reason. In that case, it makes sense.

Playing Mind Games With Yourself Time Line

It always starts the same way, "I don't want anything serious but let's just get to know each other." And you're like, "cool I don't want anything serious either, let's go with the flow."

You anticipate feelings that you do or don't even have, yet. Meaning, you don't really like the person so far, thus you feel as though everything that you feel is completely in check. Duh, because you haven't caught the deep feelings, YET.

Weeks go by and attraction increases, but you still don't want anything serious because you don't really know the person and you don't want to call it "dating" either because it makes the "flow" seem "too serious too soon." Besides, I bet one of you "just got out of a really bad relationship" huh?

You two decide to have sex and love it, so you spend a little bit more time and your emotions grow a little bit more while "being friends first and just getting to know each other."

Keep in mind, 3 months have gone by, but you two still aren't courting each other, **you're just hanging out, going with the flow, enjoying each other's time.**

About 5 months go by... Remember those emotions that you didn't have, but you said you could **control**? Yeah, they snuck up on your ass and not as easy to handle now huh? You thought you could "hold your feelings back."

My belief is that the only things you can truly hold back are your actions... But what forces are influencing those actions? The **feelings** you caught!!!!! Nevertheless, you're not together officially, and you're not making plans either. Let me guess... **"I can see you in my future so let's**

build to a relationship..."?

Now you are at 7 months of "these feelings are legit" and just want to know "what are we." Not that you want to jump into a relationship, you just want to be clear and know if the other person is on the same page because you've been acting like a real couple and rejecting your other options.

10 months go by – you two are exclusive, but not really together.

WHY NOT??? You can't say it's rushed; you can't say you're not ready. It's been 300 days of acting like a couple. How ARENT you ready? Can't say you need to work on yourself because it's been 11 months... what have you been doing? You mean to tell me you haven't worked on yourself for 12 months now? WTF.

Let's stop playing mind games with ourselves. We cannot control our emotions... They are in control of us. However, we may be able to learn to accept our emotions, and to adjust our behavioral response so that our habits no longer bother us. And the simplest way to see and make a lasting positive impact in our emotional life is to know it is not always about the emotions themselves, it's about the expression and it is about whatever we fuck around with the longest, grows.

Let's not try to
"control
our emotions"
but instead
understand
them, have
compassion for
ourselves,
and let them
be.... emotions.

Anticipating Feelings

Many of us are taken over by emotions because we are not grounded in simply being. We try to anticipate what we will or won't feel for someone. The truth is... we don't really know what we will feel after spending time with someone, thus how can we control what we haven't actually felt, yet?

It is very easy to say that we can control our anger level before we actually get upset. It is easy to say that we can control how much we love someone before we're actually in love. It is easy to say that we won't catch feelings for someone until we start hanging out with them.

The truth is, we either like people more or less depending on our time and experience with them. That's in nature's control. Only thing we control is our presence and effort. At the end of the day, we usually base our effort and presence on our emotions, anyway:

1. **The more we like people, the more we want to be around them and the more we want to show them.**

2. **The least we like people, the less we want to be around them and the less effort we put in.**

Attraction is natural. Everything else takes effort and drive. Attraction grows or fades after spending a lot time with someone. Therefore, to *control* your emotions should mean to be able to understand your feelings and not let them overwhelm your life, and to let them serve you, protect you and assist your *rational* mind.

Horacio Jones

Holding Feelings Back

Nobody shows all of their true emotions all of the time. To do so would intimately expose yourself to pain from other people. But, hiding in general is an expression of our goal to avoid vulnerability or their lack of interest in building something more. Hiding or "holding back" feelings are also acts of a coward in SOME CASES... you are not ready to take things maturely if you hide your feelings if at the same time you are still moving about like you don't have them eating you up inside.

Horacio Jones

I needed to define what being vulnerable means to me specifically.

Being vulnerable means to show myself to you completely without holding back for fear of rejection or judgment. It means to say "here I am, flaws and all. Here are my strengths, here are my weaknesses, here is where I stand – so take it or leave." Of course it is scary but I think it's also strength to conquer the fear. If vulnerability = being weak... Then I guess it takes a lot of strength to be weak.... Crazy, right?

At the end of the day, what every single one of us wants to hear is "I see you, I see all of you, I STILL love you. And want to keep loving you."

I'm looking for that balance.

Horacio Jones

Dear Feeling Hiders,

The bullshit side of "hiding feelings or holding feelings back" is that some people use the phrase as a lame excuse for why they haven't put in any effort. The fact that they paint a picture that they are afraid to love you, somehow motivates you to increase your effort to spark love in them that wasn't there before; Love that they never had. Sometimes, increasing your effort to awaken dead love within someone means that you have to compromise certain things about yourself just to accommodate them.

Think of it as over doing everything that you've been doing, and if for some reason you DO awaken the love that they've been **"holding back"**, you can't really go back to who you used to be. You have to KEEP over extending yourself and over compensating because THAT'S the version of you who they fell in love with. They fell in love with the version of you who allows them to be complacent while you do all of the relationship building alone.

YOU built the relationship, they just exist in it.

As soon as they reward you with the love that they've been **"holding back"**, you eventually invest less effort simply because you are altering back into the regular version of yourself who doesn't over extend on a daily basis, especially without the other person's same or more effort. NOW, you are demanding that they reciprocate AFTER you convinced them to give you the love that they've **held back**. But, the thing is, they fell in love without having to put in any effort.

YOU built the relationship, they just exist in it.

Dear Rejection

Anxiety and fearing rejection are feelings that will paralyze you and stop you from meeting who you really want to meet and block you from doing the things you really want to do. Don't allow anxiety and the fear of rejection to force you to come up with excuses as to why you haven't called her yet; why you haven't asked her out on a date; why you haven't sent a text; why you haven't asked to hang out.... don't be the guy who chooses to walk away from the opportunity of getting to know a great woman, the woman you're really interested in, and who runs away from asking her out. It is ok to be turned down. It is ok to feel embarrassed. If you let anxiety hold you back, it won't be the times that you made a complete fool of yourself that you will regret, but rather the times that you didn't try at something or someone out of fear.

How about this, change your perspective to understand real rejection. When you approach a woman who doesn't really know you and you want to get to know her, but she lets you know that she isn't interested.... she isn't necessarily rejecting you personally because she doesn't even know you personally. She is simply rejecting the opportunity to get to know you or just your approach.

At least now you KNOW she isn't into you. But you will never know if she is thinking of you unless you go see for yourself. That rejection is manageable.

110

True rejection happens when a woman rejects you after she has spent a considerable amount of time getting to know you. It is the ultimate rejection because at that point, you are being cut off based on your vibe and connection with her. Now that she has given it a shot at getting to know you, what she knows of you now isn't aligning with her. This means, she's not the one, and you are not her one.

When someone is trying to walk back out of the doors that that opened for you, let them.

111

Compatibility vs. Chemistry

Compatibility and chemistry are mostly ignored by dating advice because they're things that can't be faked or changed. Instead, we spend most of our time studying self-improvement and ways to "make" someone fall in love with us etc. But, you can't force Compatibility and Chemistry on another individual. The most you can do is watch how things develop and decide to make the necessary changes (or not) to make the relationship work.

The Difference

There is a big difference between chemistry and compatibility even though we use them interchangeably at times. They are words people use inaccurately to define a phantom zone or magical sentiments which exists in the space between them — the unexplainable and invisible connection. Based on my past experiences, it has been way easier to work on compatibility than it has been to work on chemistry because chemistry takes attraction aka "Sparks" and MAGIC (no clue how to find the magic potion), while compatibility takes purpose, effort, and commitment.

Compatibility is how our lifestyles, values life goals, and choices align naturally. Compatibility is based on the level of comfort with each other's character, shared experiences and the ability to have fun with each other while our lives aren't being ruined by too much sacrifices

112

or compromises. Also, compatibility usually predicts the long-term potential between two people.

Even though there is a saying, "opposites attract", high compatibility between two people comes from similarities in their standards of living and ideals. When someone says "opposites attract" they are talking about **chemistry** and how differences are "turn ons." But when you think about long term relationships, wouldn't similar views and goals (compatibility) help relationships last longer?

Think about it, famous people usually date other famous people. Christians usually date other Christians. Simply because people of opposite moral values (compatibility) will literally push each other away over time, even when they have great sex and attraction (chemistry). When two people's lifestyles are similar, it is easier to make long term plans. Let's say a preacher dates a stripper. They may have chemistry, but they would have to do a lot of compromising, changing and sacrificing to make things work.

On the other hand, a lack of chemistry doesn't result in two people **pushing** each other away; it simply results in a lack of attraction, sex, and "magic". And the final outcome is that things feel forced, dead and boring. So, instead of repelling each other when there is no chemistry (magic), two people usually **drift** away from each other slowly.

113

High level of chemistry yields emotional warmth, sexual attraction and comfort with being open about feelings. It is usually considered as the magic that drives relationships for a short period of time, but the lack of compatibility may cause frustration and can definitely blow out the "magical sparks."

I have found that in order to measure how compatible you are, just look at how much sacrificing and compromising you have to do, and how much conflict they cause. The more compatible you are the less natural urges you have to compromise on. The less compatible you are, the more sacrifices you have to make.

This would reveal why so many of us "don't want anything serious." We are used to forcing compatibility with someone after being serious and it back fires: over compromising, over sacrificing = feeling like relationships hold us back, lock us down and are too much work. We stay in those "complicated" relationships because of the chemistry, not because of the compatibility.

Ever met someone who is compatible with you: stable job, good person, healed, respectful, ambitious etc... But there was no "chemistry"? And you decided NOT to date them because there was no Spark?

So, why would you date someone who has the spark and chemistry but are not compatibility with you?

Random Chemistry Thoughts

Matter cannot be
created
or destroyed.
I often wonder...
is love the same?

*People are more willing
to work on a relationship
if the issue is compatibility
because chemistry fuels
them.*

*But if there is no spark,
most people jump ship*

Has chemistry always existed
Between two people
In one form or the other?

I heard that it is chemistry when
you find someone who makes
you feel how you *want* to feel

Potential Isn't Unique

Falling for someone's potential sums up the story of relationships for so many of us. We unintentionally set ourselves up for heartbreak by falling in love with the potential of someone instead of looking at who they are right now.

However, it is also such a great quality we hold. We have this extremely optimistic and positive outlook that we apply to people we're interested in. We first meet them as just the person they are in front of us that day, but then we perceive so much of what and who they can be **if only** they could **"see our worth."**

Our ability to see beyond someone's faults and see their full potential is truly a beautiful thing. We feel so motivated to display this whole other side of life by having sex, cooking, paying, supporting and showing them our higher level of love. We are so excited to be that perfect person that they never had before and to show them how wonderful their life can be with our love. There's absolutely nothing wrong with fantasizing about the romantic possibilities like that until it stops you from accepting reality.

Re: We fall in love with our own ideas of people.

What Is Potential?

Potential is just potential! Possibilities, likelihoods,

imaginations, misconceptions, illusions, odds, fantasies, fancies… It's not that unique at all if you think about it. Everyone has potential. I have potential, you have potential, the man across the street, the person who cuts your hair, your ex, the McDonald's employee. Everyone has it. We all have potential to be better people, or worse people. It's just there. So what is so special about that certain person's potential that has you all caught up and head over heels?

Make It Real

Until two people SHOW and say, "we're officially together," they can have all the potential in the world — but a relationship isn't necessarily going to happen. Potential is there but **not moving**. Accordingly, when you make the decision to be in a relationship with someone, to get things **moving**, it is assumed that you are agreeing to accept the person for who they are and work through any issues together. That agreement **moves things forward**. When you admit to being official, you're no longer a "potential relationship," you now are committed to an actual relationship. You made it real and not just a possibility.

War On Potential

Potential puts pressure on both people. It can lead to resentment if someone doesn't match up to that potential version. Maybe you are constantly pushing them to change into someone they are not, complaining about the same things over and over, only to be disappointed time and time again simply because the potential that you want them to be is different from who they are today and who THEY want to be. Or maybe someone feels as though you aren't trying hard enough to be who they want you to be - you would feel like nothing you do will ever be enough.

Having to compete with "potential" can have you feeling inadequate, not good enough, judged and criticized. It can actually be very damaging. This happens because they could be smothering you by chasing some future version of you that doesn't exist, so you have no room to be your authentic self; they could be indirectly making you feel as though you are not good enough as you are. That's not exactly going to make you want to be around them. It makes them appear to want ANY relationship at any cost, even if it's not what YOU want. They unconsciously tip the balance for you to compete with "potential" but often end up blaming YOU for having "commitment phobia" - no, you're just not happy competing against the "future" you, for them.

If you see something in someone that they do not see in themselves that can help **THEM**, give them love so that they can see what you see. If you see something in them that's going to make THEM a better person for **THEMSELVES**, I think **that's** driven by **Love**. And you just want to see THEM do better in life for **THEMSELVES** and you'll be happy about those changes they'll make for **THEMSELVES**. But if all you can see is the potential for them to change in order to make YOU happy, that's selfishness. You want them to change things about themselves because they don't make **you** happy. But, they haven't changed those things for a reason. They do what they do because they want to do it.

Dear Desire,

I am the way that I am because I generally **desire** to be this way. The potential that you see is different from the potential that I see. If you haven't loved me for who I am today yet, how can you love me for who I can be in some future day that doesn't exist? Accept me as I am.

Think about this, people are a certain way because they want to be, and choose to be. There are certain changes that they want to make for **THEMSELVES**, but for the most part, people do what the hell they want to do because that's how the f*** they want to be and that's what the f*** they want to do. That's who they are, and you can't keep letting "potential" keep you from accepting that.

Now, when you want someone to stop doing something, do something more, do something different, act another way and it's something that they just don't want to do, you're asking that person to be someone else for YOU because it'll make YOU happier. There is a reason why after all of that complaining you've been doing, they haven't transformed into that type of person. They don't want to make those changes because that's just not who they are or who they want to be. Have you ever asked yourself why they won't make the changes? Will those changes make THEM happy or just make YOU happy?

I AM THE LOVE OF MY LIFE

How NOT To Fall For Potential

The answer is that it's a balance. It's about keeping this beautiful quality being able to see someone as more, while at the same time reminding ourselves that we really don't know this person enough or that this person actually has to become that future version BEFORE we allow ourselves to fall for it. So we stop ourselves from getting emotionally and physically involved with someone until enough time (it depends on how long you choose to wait) has passed for them to show us what they are all about. Why? Because it is possible that they will never become the potential version that WE SEE.

We do this by keeping the focus on ourselves, not becoming exclusive without truly being official, still living our lives, and not allowing our imaginations to run wild with dreams and plans of the relationship UNTIL THEY HAVE MADE IT CLEAR THAT THEY WANT to travel the same path as we do.

Do you get what I'm saying? It's not easy to slow ourselves down when our hearts have so much love to give and we sooooo want this to be it, and them to be the one. We can fantasize about them to be the one as long as we don't let the fantasy cloud the reality.

When is it okay?

Support is acceptable. Pushiness is not. Everyone chooses to change in his or her own time and on his or her own terms. Before judging someone, criticizing or pressuring them to change, take a good hard look at yourself. Are you perfect? Are you everything this person wants and needs? Potential is appropriate when their current actions align with their own plan and vision for who THEY want to be.

How many times do we hear people say: "It's not the same anymore, you've changed." The truth is, that person was putting on a show and now their show has ended: their true self appeared when they started to become complacent.

Moving on
was like
building
a new
home...
big enough
for only
myself
my wounds
and my healing.

Horacio Jones

#HJNOTES

You can start moving on whenever you want to. I had my heart broken and I thought that I would never be able to move on. However, one day I realized that I am the only person able to deal and manage how I feel! I am the love of my life. I understood that I would never be able to change the fact that what happened had hurt me, but accepting it and learning from it was what helped me to move on. Why stress for only one person if there are tons of others out there just waiting to receive the love that someone else didn't want?

Moving On

The other day, I was thinking... I would hate to start all over with someone new, create thousands of beautiful memories, just for those same memories to come back and hunt me after a break up. Of course I wouldn't enter into a relationship that I didn't feel would last, but I have to be realistic: sometimes shit happens and people break up after truly believing "I met the one". Those memories are so dope and pleasant during their creation, but later down the road when you revisit those same memories after a break up, they hurt like hell. Remember how fun it was on those late night trips to get food together? Now, you don't even want to think about it. Something that always gets to me personally is when I hear the "In The Morning" song by J. Cole and Drake. It doesn't matter when or where I hear it, I just instantly think of an ex. Why? Because that's the song that I used as her ring tone on my phone when she called. It is not that I miss that ex, it's just that the song in particular triggers memories of her. Random people, places and things spark memories out of nowhere and there are some memories that are randomly triggered with a more emotional effect than others.

I AM THE LOVE OF MY LIFE

The most important thing that I've learned while studying psychology in college, is that **our memories aren't always fair to our hearts...** THATS why it's so hard to move on.... we remember exes, and our emotions are conditioned to our memories. If we could simply forget, we wouldn't feel shit. Think about it, we are hurting because we remember the betrayal and we constantly replay it over and over in our minds. But, if we could somehow snap our fingers and forget the whole relationship and person, there would be no more pain as we'd have no memory of what caused it. It would be so simple.

Remember?

I don't believe it is a bad thing to remember, still love and care for someone without it negatively affecting our love lives with other people. If the relationship is over; we have exhausted the methods and different ways of reconciling; all communication has stopped, you can still have a special place in my mind.

Memories and emotions are two of the reasons why we maintain anger, happiness and everything else, even love for people. We may not be able to forget them, but something that we can look forward to is that as time pass, the pain associated with the memories become dull, especially when we make new memories with new people.

What if we remembered our exes every time we pass by an old restaurant that we went to and instead of avoiding it, we went inside with love ones and created many new beautiful memories? Now, every time we pass by that restaurant, we'll remember the newer memories and less about our exes.

How To Move On

Let's choose space and time away to figure out appropriate healing habits and THEN date NEW people. Staying with someone is a choice and so is moving on. Don't forget that dealing with a break up can open doors to self-love, making you more confident, and as a result, a better person.

Nonetheless, the thing is, when you have truly loved someone, they never leave you. They live inside you... they have a home in your brain. You can try to ignore and deny this, and probably you can repress it and "forget them", but I would suggest trying to create a kind of mental room in your mind where that person can still live because all of those memories of happiness and of what was lost can remind you of a beautiful time in your life and how you gained strength from the break up... without it affecting your new days because you don't hate anyone or desire them anymore; you humbly just remember them.

Make up your mind and stick to it: Make a choice. Either run from the pain or deal with it. Moving on is a decision you make and STAY dedicated to. Even if your emotions are strong, you can still decide to move on. You can't backtrack or else it's going to take forever. Once you get the physical things moving on, you open up the lane for your emotions to move on too. Which means all of that physical shit ceases: text and calls, sex, stalking social media. Stick to your decision even when you start missing them. Or else the memories will stay fresh. Rise up to the challenge and deal with it directly. This will allow you to be free of the pain in the time it takes rather than lingering on it forever.

Time: "time" alone isn't going to cut it. It's what you do with that time. You have no control over time but it is a gift. Spend it alone. Spend it away. Spend it listening to music that will put you in the mood that you WANT to be in. Spend it doing things you actually like doing alone. Why? So that you can get used to being by yourself again; used to enjoying your own presence, your own space. Healing WILL take a long *time*.

Space: having your own space is dope. You have so much control over your own solitude. But, that can't happen if your ex is always in the way. Think of it as having to restart your moving on process every time you reply, see them and have sex... you're extending the time that it would take to move on because you're not truly experiencing life in space without them. After you are comfortable in your space, you are allowed to let someone *new* in.

Healing Habits: Healing habits are things that you start doing to improve yourself. Most of these things will of course be hard to commit to because your desire to do them may not be there. For example, NOT texting your ex. You WILL have the urge to talk to them and even create reasons to contact them. Create a new habit to replace replying to them. When you get the urge to hit them up, find something else to do. Not just anything else, do something productive. That way, even while hurting, you're still building.

Pause before
you lie to
yourself

Stop
Breaking
Your
Own
Rules

I AM THE LOVE OF MY LIFE

Dear self,

It is extremely unpleasant to let go of true love, and that is precisely why I think we shouldn't have to let go of it. Instead, we could release the **person**, while still caring for them from a great distance concurrently developing more power to continue on with our lives. We can forgive ourselves and release them by pursuing a better version of ourselves.

Letting go and latching onto new things are necessary parts of life. Everyone will tell you to "keep yourself busy, focus on other things, do this do that, don't even think of him/her" But frankly speaking, you already know all this, don't you?

Everyone will tell you a whole bunch of impractical nonsense like "STOP thinking about them"... and you know that it is bullshit and annoying advice. You want to know HOW to stop thinking about them if that's even possible. You want to hear something way more straightforward: This shit is going to hurt like hell for a long ass time. So, what I suggest is nothing unique.

Just ask yourself: Do you want to spend the rest of your life thinking about it and feeling bad because it ended? Or do you want to keep it as an old good memory and grow from it? I think that the most important thing to remember during a breakup is that you really have to accept your thoughts and memories, not fight them.

We should try to understand that just because one person betrays us, it doesn't mean that we're unworthy of love from other people.

Sometimes, love means letting go and being happy about not hating anyone.

Communicating with exes to tell them that we're not communicating with them IS communicating with them!! As long as we respond, they won't leave us alone. EVERY time we text back, we are guaranteeing they will too.

Dear self,

Start physically moving on today. You don't know how far you will have to walk. But you know that if you turn around now, the move on process restarts and you never get to restart from where you left off.

When moving on, it's all about when and where you start and how long you can keep walking in that opposite direction. You can start now, here, today. Just start physically moving things so that your emotions can have a clear lane to move on as well.

You probably won't be able to delete all of the pictures, but delete some. You probably won't be able to ignore them, but try spending less time replying. Whatever you focus on, grows. Focus on creating distance between you and what's holding you back.

Moving on
is just the
movement
from fighting
and ignoring
the truth to
accepting it.

Horacio Jones

The most
important thing
about loving
yourself
is that you
can keep
doing it
after
someone
else
stops

Horacio Jones

Letting Go Vs. Giving Up

Letting go and "giving up" are two very different things. When we let go, we accept that things aren't working out and decide to explore life without investing any more into that person. We still care and wish them the best, but we're choosing to focus on ourselves. It means having the strength and maturity to understand what is important and what isn't after giving it an HONEST try.

When we Let go, it means accepting an obstacle and not letting the situation make a victim out of us after giving it a STRAIGHTFORWARD try to work things out.

"We tried our best, but now I would like to try something else without you because it isn't working out. I wish you good luck with everything. I am ready to take on new goals."

When you're giving up, you're thinking,

"I can't f****** do this s*** anymore. F*** you. It's all your fault. I hate you. I will never find anyone else. I'm damaged. I'm broken."

I AM THE LOVE OF MY LIFE

Dear self,

The big difference between giving up on someone and letting go is accepting them for who they are. When you give up on someone, you believe that there is no hope for them to be who YOU want them to be; you can't accept them as they are. But, when you let go, you believe there is hope for them to be better generally, just not for you and you're no longer waiting for them... but you still care... from a distance.

Perspective: Letting go is knowing that if what you want is meant to be, it will happen without you over pushing it if you've done what you can do already on your end. Giving up is when you haven't given it your all because it's too much for you and you love the potential of someone more than the reality. To "let go" is to MOVE ON and allow yourself enough energy to take on the next hurdle in front of you because you don't want to exhaust yourself on someone who will not serve you any good. Giving up is when there are ways through a problem but you're not trying to find a way simply because you are too hurt and angry.

Letting go is accepting that you cannot do something right now. You choose to let this moment go and MAY try again later. The flow continues. Giving up is justifying why you can never do something and there is no question of retrying. The flow stops.

When you **let go** of someone, you know that they do not affect you and you will be ok without them. You let go of people with a sense of knowing you'll be fine. When people **give up**, they do not know what else to do. They worry more about the victim.

Letting go means that you are optimistic. It's a sign of how positive you are about your future. You know this particular person might not be the way that you want them after fairly trying, so you let them go and wish yourself someone better. No hate for the ex though. Giving up means you are pessimistic. You only see the negative part of holding on. And you are going to constantly whine about it your whole life. You're bitter and HATE your ex and won't stop trying to make them care about hurting you.

142

Sometimes,
you pray
for growth
but reject it
when it means you
have to let go of a
specific person.
That's because
you allow the
person to become
more important
than your growth.

Horacio Jones

I AM THE LOVE OF MY LIFE

Dear Self,

Don't allow someone else's potential to be more important than yours if it's destroying you. Don't allow someone else's chaos be more vital than yours if it's infecting you. Sometimes, it's better to let them GO so that you can grow.

Sometimes, people become rocks, boulders or mountains in our lives... Not the kind that embodies strength and stability, but the kind that blocks our growth; the kind that's in our way, distracting us and bringing us down.

When we notice how heavy things have gotten, we ask God to cut any dead weight from our lives, and we start noticing that we'll lose some "friends" but gain better friends. Some family may fade away while we grow closer to other family members. We'll lose a job and end up at a way better one. We may fail a class but switch majors and become a boss at school. Blessing start to flow in because we accept that some things and people have to go away in order for better people and things to come along.

But, the moment we start losing "our lover"... we panic, so we hold on. We're not ready to let them go. We don't want to keep going if it means we can't take our lovers with us. All of a sudden, we start underperforming at work and missing out on promotions and missing school assignments. We start missing out on blessing because they can't wait any longer. All of our blessing start running away from us simply because we want our lovers to change more than we want God to set us free.

Let go!

Horacio Jones

144

Dear Self,

Not a single person is
  born to be alone.
   But, just so we are clear,
if you're by your lonesome now,
  just look in the mirror.
Love who you see and you
  will discover that love in
someone else.
I know it seems difficult to do,
  but also I know that,
    you have what it takes.
  Go... love yourself without stopping.
   Hold on to who you really are.
    Stop counting the roses that
never came.
You deserve the love that
you have given.
  Remember this day...
when you refused to settle for less.
  when you chose to be
the love of your life, and

I, The Love Of Mine

X Horacio Jones

145

It is easy to walk
away but tougher
to stay away...

Both are
CHOICES.

I *can* choose.

Which one am
I more afraid
of losing, *you* or
myself?

If I have lost myself
with you, I can surely
find myself
without you...

this is how to let you
go and to stay away...

to find myself doing
better without you.

Horacio Jones

Forgiveness
Doesn't
Always
Equal
Reconciliation

Dear self,

While forgiveness is important, a "notice" should be added. Forgiveness doesn't always equal reconciliation. It does not always bring two people back together.

While forgiveness is good for us, we shouldn't always invite toxic people back into our lives. Even with time, some people simply don't ever change their behavior.

Just because we forgave someone doesn't mean we forgot what type of toxic person they are.

Trying to force forgiveness is unwise.

Dear self,

How do you forgive someone who is constantly trying to hurt you, manipulate you, use you, and lie to you? How do you forgive someone who doesn't ask for forgiveness or show any guilt? Do they deserve your sympathy, love, and kindness? If you forgive a person who thinks it's ok to constantly fuck you over or play dumb when confronted, is it worth lowering your standards to let them back in after forgiving them?

Fuck No!

That's why after forgiving people, you should set new boundaries to prevent them from infiltrating your healing and block them from inflicting more pain on you. You need to set a boundary of protection which is a path to healing rather than using "forgiveness" as a mask to allow bad behavior to be accepted and allowed.

You deserve peace after what someone has put you through. And the only way to get it is to continue to live life, try to help others exceed their own painful life experiences, and keep toxic people away.

I AM THE LOVE OF MY LIFE

The person who hurt me may never feel guilty, but I have no control over that. I only control my own actions. And I can choose peace and acceptance to move forward. Or I can choose to hold onto the pain and anguish over what they did. But, each day, I try to choose peace and trust that the Universe will bring good people and blessings my way as life goes on.

Horacio Jones

Dear Forgiveness,

Forgiveness is not something we do for another person. Forgiveness is something we give ourselves. If we have been wronged, the last thing we want to do is carry that burden with us forever, right? Let that shit go.

Pain doesn't last forever. Give yourself time to heal. I promise you it does get easier with time. But, I get it, when it comes to letting go and forgiving someone, it sometimes feels like they "got away with it" or that they "are let off way too easily." All it takes is a switch in perspective to obliterate that feeling.

Is forgiveness necessary?

I was used to accepting that holding a grudge stops me from enjoying my life, assuming that I needed to forgive someone completely to let go of that grudge. Then, I realized that often times, only SOME forgiveness is enough for me. And that there's no need to allow that person to affect me anymore. No need to let them back in. I can be happy without them. I can let go of what someone has done to me without also having to forget and give them another chance to hurt me again.

Here is the perspective switch: **We rarely forgive anyone completely.** Therefore, we can let go of that grudge just as we let go of any other harmful thought without the need to forgive by accepting that we can heal and recover because forgiveness isn't about letting **them** off of the hook, it's about letting ourselves off of the hook.

Forgiveness doesn't always make everything better and I can't do it when I'm not ready. If I'm hurting, it's hard to see anything else but the pain and unfortunately, saying that I forgive someone will not take the pain away. I have to get to the point where I choose healing and moving forward instead of pain regardless if I forgave them or not.

One day you'll realize that you are stuck in one place while everything and everyone has moved on. Not because you haven't forgiven someone, but because you haven't fully focused on healing. Once you get to that point, you can begin to consider forgiveness. It's not easy, there is no time limit on when or why but when you're tired of carrying the burden of pain, you can start moving on.

why is it difficult to forgive
someone who has wronged you?

We believe they would have an
easy way out if we forgive them.

We believe they would be walking
away freely.

We believe they deserve our
pettiness,
   hatred
   and
   anger.

It makes us feel superior.

We behave like a victim and enjoy
self-sympathy and empathy from
others

There are
people who
I have let
go of and
have not
forgiven...
who are not
causing me
any pain
because I
healed the
parts of me
that
wanted
them.

Horacio Jones

#HealBeforeYouDeal

I would hate for my love to be so loud and booming to a point where you can't hear your own heart; to the point where you ignore your own love and Journey. I would hate for my tenderness to distract you or knock you off of your own course in life. I would hate for my lips to make you forget about your own or I would hate it if the way I looked at you made you stop looking at yourself in your own unique way. I would hate for you to think that you "can't live without me". I don't want to "complete you". I want to be extra pieces in your love. I want you to be whole with or without me.

I don't want my love to side track you. I don't want my effort to knock you off balance or unhinge you because it would suck to be so in love with someone who forgets to love themselves. Neither one of us deserves that.

What I do to show you how much I love you is distracting. See, I naturally want to be a giver, a supporter... Your extra encouragement and motivation. I have this intense urge to push you to love yourself... To try to spark something in you to help "fix" you or "save" you.

But, then again, I get it, shoving my love, my worth, my journey down your throat won't always work. You may need your OWN healing space; your own track to focus on loving yourself more, not loving me more.

If I had to walk away in order for you to love yourself, I'd be doing it because I love you.... And if you wanted to love me better, you'll learn to love yourself better. This is not an invitation to pretend to love yourself, or hide insecurities just to keep me around. I am releasing you.

Dear Self,

If you have personal scars that are not yet healed, you have to work on you because anyone you touch can either be poisoned by your brokenness or healed by your wholeness.

A little fear is normal, but don't let fear paralyze you into not living and not healing. Singleness is a phase of self-love and self-discovery, but it is still a phase and life is about evolving mentally, spiritually and physically and knowing when the season has changed. Singleness is about grasping your truth and relationships are about surrendering to your truth. Let someone into your space after you heal and watch the dimension change. Where there is joy, there is pain and where there is love the possibility of hurt and brokenness lingers, but the possibility of beauty and transformation lingers as well.

Feelings come in waves

Dear Broken,

You are not broken. You are breaking through!!! Positive self-talk changes how you see yourself. When you are hurt, you FEEL broken into pieces. Your heart feels fractured in millions of places, each one dangerously cracking out of control, cutting anyone who tries to "save" you. It feels like you're scattered all over the floor.

Pick yourself up. Love each piece. Throw away what you don't want. Add new significant pieces. Heal.

Your natural state is wholeness, singular. By labeling yourself in a negative way, you are making yourself less and psychologically forcing yourself to take on the qualities of being incomplete, "broken", "having trust issues", "insecure", "worthless."

By using positive self-talk, you prepare yourself for a more optimistic journey to love yourself. Just try it. Changing what you say and think about yourself helps restore you to balance.

I am not broken, I am rediscovering myself. I am the love of my life. That's so dope!!!!

160

Fuck Love?

Saying fuck love is like saying fuck what cures me or fuck what makes me feel good. But, love always feels good. Love provides you with everything your soul needs. Love makes you feel the beauty of the world around you. A smile from a lover makes you happy. When you feel it, you know it. It is like no other feeling in the world that I know of and has the power to make everything else (literally everything) secondary. Real love allows you to be who you really are. Real love allows you the freedom to express yourself and grow as a human being.

It doesn't manipulate you or exploit your mind. It doesn't cheat on you for temporary pleasure. Love commits to you, protects you and constantly tries to do better by you.

Love heals hurt and kills hate.

If you think love sucks, it's because you haven't discovered the real problem. I know that love sometimes feels like all of the other crazy drugs kids are doing these days but love is not hurting you... Not having who you want in the way that you want them is what hurts you. Not trusting who you have is what hurts. Being lied to hurts.

Another issue could be how your belief about "love sucks" blending with other emotions that add to the pain.

I AM THE LOVE OF MY LIFE

I AM THE LOVE OF MY LIFE

Fear.
Anger.
Helplessness.
Loneliness.
Jealousy.

Those aren't feelings of love.
Those are feelings of the lack of love.

"Don't stop loving yourself just to love me. Neither one of us deserves that

Horacio Jones

Sometimes, we forget to listen to all parts of ourselves like our mind, soul and body. We get lost or confused by only following the heart.

Horacio Jones

Fake Fine

Some of us are experts at pretending that we're fine. I get it… It's very hard to face the truth. But, you're not fine. Period. It'll become much easier to accept the fact that you've lost someone you love and it'll be much easier to move on once you stop trying to conceal it. The more you pretend to be fine and tell yourself so, the harder it will be to actually transition into the stage of being REAL single, not FAKE single.

Real-single is when you don't feel like you're cheating on your ex by dating someone new. Or when you are concerned about your own shit, not your ex's other lovers.

Fake-single is when you're still being a hell of a relationship partner to someone who's not with you. You turn down better people because you're "loyal" to and ex. You still have sex with your ex because you are lonely, horny and only comfortable with them. You don't go on any dates; you don't focus on your own life. But you put on a big smile in front of everyone saying "I'm just working on myself."

Let yourself mourn. Cry. Write. Surround yourself with friends who listen, not the ones who stroke your victimization ego like "fuck them, you deserve better. It's all **their** fault. They ain't shit". Because the truth is, you probably "ain't shit" either and only deserve better when you heal better. The temptation may be to pretend you're unaffected by the breakup; don't let pride get in the way of being real so you can heal. If you are hurting, be **real-hurt** and not **fake-healed.**

Fake-Healed

Just like someone can be "Fake Fine", they can also pretend to be completely healed from the past. You might feel confused, afraid, alone, sad, or betrayed. You might want to say fuck it and just give up and move on, or you may want to stick around and stay for a little while longer to see if things will get better. And those are all normal, natural feelings to have when the "relationship" is coming to an end or when it's at a bad place.

But, let's say you end it, then spend time alone. And you don't want anyone new to notice your pain because, let's face it, brokenness sucks. There's no denying it. I know because I've been there too many times. So, I understand what this feels like.

You KNOW you're not healed but you want some attention and sex in your life again, so you put up a front as if you are all fine so that potential dates won't run from you thinking you are too damaged to date. Let's stop this bullshit. It's annoying.

Yo, if you start dating as a **Fake-Healed** person because you are lonely, the brokenness and self-sabotage of new relationships will continue and hinder you from healing unless you actively try to **heal for YOU before you try to deal with someone else.** So, please stop faking like shit isn't bothering you still. Please stop faking like you trust people. Don't fake it just because you are afraid of pushing them away. Don't be **fake-healed** just to get "play time" in the bed room.

No one wants to deal with your surprise trust issues or controlling behavior a few months from now. Eventually, they will discover the truth because you become so overloaded with "excess" emotions that all of the bullshit comes flowing out in the form of trust issues, insecurities, lies, manipulation, jealousy, and passive aggressiveness because you can't fake it or hold it back forever.

Dear self,

Be REAL-Hurt because it's important to be in touch with your real emotions. Avoiding them or finding reasons not to connect with yourself can cause you to hide from your feelings. Then spaz out on whoever it is you're trying to "fake-healed" date.

Without working through your emotions and allowing yourself to feel, you're not going to be able to heal. I'm telling you. Your pain will slip through the cracks and have someone else calling you "crazy" because you took all of that baggage and slowly dumped it on them because it was too much to hide and hold inside.

Let that shit go and heal for REAL.

Fake Break Up

When people fail to understand the incompatibility because they want you to act a certain way, they become very petty and manipulative and pretend to want to break up with you. Lord knows I hate the "Fake Break up" manipulation technique when they break up to make up instead of breaking up to break up. Some people break up because they think it will catapult the other person into changing, appreciating them more and putting in more effort. They want you to feel what life is like without them so that you would try harder to keep them.

Don't fall into this trap. Not only is it manipulation and game playing but it is likely to backfire quickly. Eventually, people realized the pettiness and they will stop chasing after every temper tantrum.

If you do it often enough or keep threatening to leave, they will get fed up with your little game and let your ass leave. If you want to break up because you're not getting your way or because you're not getting what you want out of the relationship, then LEAVE! And stay gone... Because we know you're only breaking up in the hopes that your absence from our lives will suddenly "make us see" that you are 'the one'. No. That's not how you communicate in a healthy manner.

Most times, threatening to leave doesn't get people to change because they know damn well you're not serious about breaking up and that you're not really going anywhere. People who want to break up, will break up, and stay broken up. Stop fronting and faking.

Once you have to resort to manipulation just to get someone to be the way that you want them to be, that might be the perfect time to leave FOR REAL because you can't change people. Manipulation is abuse, not love.

Insecurities can turn you into a monster.

Dear self,

beware of dating extremely insecure people. They are very controlling, sensitive, and their insecurities will force them to constantly push to find everything wrong with you just because they can't see anything right within themselves.

Horacio Jones

I don't want to become the type of person who starts to believe that attachment leads to unhappiness based on a few past heartbreaks.

I don't think you should strive to be detached. I think you should pay careful attention to your attachments and let them go when they are no good for you, heal, then attach to better things.

Horacio Jones

Shade

First, what is passive aggressiveness? A LEARNED trifling communication style used by someone who chooses to act like they have an inability to deal with their own bitterness, anger, and whatever the hell is REALLY bothering them, in a healthy manner. They use a passive form of hostility and indirect acts of aggression. They passively do something specifically to piss someone off, and hide behind the phrase "I didn't mean it like that, you must be guilty of something if you're reacting like that". They say that they are just joking and it takes away your power and right to get mad by it. Then it becomes your problem because you are being so "sensitive." It's annoying and exhausting.

Passive aggressiveness is a defense mechanism that allows people who aren't comfortable being openly aggressive to still piss you off by **throwing shade**: saying something derogatory about another person, or belittling them in an underhanded fashion.

Passive Aggressive behavior aka being petty aka throwing shade is the kind of behavior people choose (some don't know they act this way) when they feel unable to openly express their unhappiness or anger about something. They intentionally say one thing and do another, just to make you feel some type of way, and when you react, they blame you for starting the argument. They intentionally sabotage situations to upset you or get back at you. It's simple, they fear the consequences of open conversations and being straight forward so if things hit the fan, they won't be blamed for it.

Talking to a person who uses petty passive aggressiveness is hard because they usually deny that they are doing anything. They frustrate you so much until you get totally upset and then throw it in your face like "why are you getting so mad, it's not even that serious." Since they may not have good communication skills, they can't handle your directness, so they throw "low blows" to get their points across.

They don't get it though. When you date someone who is so petty and immature, they always have you on the guessing game, trying to read their mind because they're so indirect. You end up feeling shut down, ignored or like YOU'RE the one who is "tripping and don't know how to act." They know that at some point, you will explode, then blame you to gain the upper hand.

People become more passive aggressive if they don't open the hell up and try to express themselves. For a lot of people, being passive-aggressive is the only way to show their feelings. They fear conflict, so when you get angry, they get too uncomfortable... therefore their aggression gets even more buried, and expressed in more hidden ways.

In my personal experience passive aggressive people are immature and don't understand that working things out means talking without hidden aggression.

Dear Rescuers,

Beware of the desperate rescuers of the world. They only pursue hurt people and jump in to try and "save the day". They obsess over fixing people.

They look for "needy" people because they have a "hero" complex. They feel the need to save someone, fix them, then mold them into greatness. One huge reason to constantly seek out someone "damaged" is so they can mask their own issues. Therefore, anyone who is searching for someone they can "save" is in need of some salvation as well.

These "heroes" seek out people with a whole bunch of emotional baggage. Their goal is to "repair" them and then to keep them locked up afterwards, like: "I MADE YOU. IF IT WASN'T FOR ME... BLAH". These rescuers act like they're helping you out and getting you to open up then turn right around and criticize you for it or hold it against you in the end. Once they gain trust, they can easily hold those insecurities against you, bringing up all of that past shit that they know hurts you the most so that they can keep the upper hand.

It's a way of gaining control over you. That's why you need to think twice about who you are spilling your pain to because people will use it as a weapon. Every time you want to leave, they make you feel worthless. They try to make you think that you would be nothing without them. As you can guess, it's nearly impossible to be equals in a

177

relationship where someone considers themselves to be your "hero."

Don't let anyone come in and claim that they "saved you." It's YOUR healing and YOUR life.

> **I often feel empowered and motivated while single but threatened by insecurity and stress when in relationships. And I think that's why I cherish the single life so much. I know that won't break my own heart**

I won't break my own heart. I'm great being single. There are of course lonely nights but all manageable. However, once I'm with someone, the upsets of lonely nights are intensified. I hate feeling uneasy. I don't feel those things until I start liking someone. It's like, once you open your heart up for love, all of the other emotions flood out too. I don't like worrying and wondering. I don't like feeling as though in order to like someone with all the happy emotions, the bad ones have to consume me first. When I'm single and to myself, I don't feel any of that. I think it's an insecurity. Because I feel like I'm perfect and enough for myself, but may not be enough for someone else.

Maybe it's my body telling me "you shouldn't be here." A defense mechanism, self-preservation because I've been hurt or disappointed before. Once I begin to like someone and begin to get close, I tend to notice and concentrate on their flaws instead of their positive aspects. And I am torn between the instinct that tells me that they're no good and the insecurity that tells me that they are good, but I'm not.

**No one ever wants
to admit how easy
it is to drown in
their memories**

Dear Memories,

The smallest things trigger old memories

The thing is, old wounds have a way of resurfacing as we fall again, learn, and grow. Is that a bad thing altogether? Nope. It's called strength, to be able to move forward while having constant reminders of what "used to be" everywhere around you.

Remembering exes doesn't make us weak. It makes us human. We don't need to let go of anything forever. We just need to learn what it means to let go in a moment, and then remember what that looks and feels like to do it again when necessary.

Closure

Closure isn't always something that we find outside of ourselves. I think that most times, we need to find our own closure in our own selves, especially if our ex love ones aren't willing to help us with it.

But, why do we want closure so badly? For many of us, closure is the feeling of completion. Done. Finished. Everything addressed and understood. Also, healing seems lighter when you can talk about why your relationship ended. But unfortunately, we don't always get the closer that we think we deserve or that we think we need in order to move on, so we stick around for answers instead of moving on.

We end up feeling emptier, angrier and more confused or stuck, waiting for more answers. We want to know more about when did their feelings change, where, how, and why did they do what they did. Can we fix it? Are they willing to fix it? Were we not enough? Did we do too much? Was it all a lie? Was it our fault...

You tell yourself that all you want is to express your thoughts and feelings and try and make sense of what went wrong and why it happened, so that you can either fix things or learn from the experience and avoid making the same mistakes in future relationships. But, you won't fully accept that not every question needs an answer right now and those unanswered questions can have you waiting forever for closure, even when it does not really

181

serve you well. Sometimes, "I need closure" is actually just an excuse to hold on.

Understand the harsh reality, sometimes, people leave you and do not reply to your calls, text messages, they block you, they move on to someone else. They don't want anything to do with you anymore. Sometimes, you don't get the closure in the form of words... That's when you have to accept it based on their actions.

Think about it, after everything you have been through with someone, they leave you hurt, confused, alone and in a mess to deal with on your own.... And that's exactly what you should do... Deal with that shit on your own. THAT'S your closure. For the simple fact that they won't even speak to you to address anything, should let you know how much they really care now. It's not about how they USED to care... They don't care NOW!!

So, do you still think that you need their closure?

When we are looking for closure from the other person, we are also seeking validation, confirmation and a possible resolution with them. Learning to "self-close the fucking door" is a great gift. YOU close it. It's your door. Your ex doesn't have to give you closure, but YOU **have** to give yourself closure. Closure is permission to move on, but you can actually grant that to yourself. YOU need to give YOU permission to move on. Close **your** door.

I AM THE LOVE OF MY LIFE

Most times I think we're actually better off not obsessing over seeking closure with someone else because while it opens the door for SOME clarity, it also opens the door for them to bullshit us even more and to manipulate us into staying. Again…. Their ending behavior, the way they leave things with us, should be all the closure we ever need. Close **your** door.

Our theory is that closure is going to give us peace or calm us down so that we can accept things and move on. If we know the who, what, when, where, how and why things went wrong with someone, then maybe we would know what we can improve upon, and MOVE ON.

At the end of the day, isn't all we want after a breakup is to accept it and move on? To let that shit go and move on? To leave the bullshit of the past behind us and move on?

If yes, then seek **"self-closure."** It's wayyyyyy better than waiting for closure from someone else. Let's be honest, the real reason the relationship didn't work out is most likely something you are better off not even hearing or knowing.

Thinking of "closure", it's about closing the door to your past which essentially doesn't exist anymore; so all of your power and purpose to "know when, where, how, who, when and why", is in this present moment, dragging problems from the past and only bringing you down.

Let that shit go.

Opening the door for "closure" also opens the door for more BULLSHIT and manipulation.

The relationship didn't work out because it just wasn't meant to be or the timing was off. Do you really want to reopen old wounds with pieces of closure you can obsess over for the next year? Hell no. You're never going to be able to have all the answers as to why things didn't work out.

1. **Trust**: Friendships build trust with someone before we jump into being serious with them. The person we're in a relationship with becomes our best friend, and if we can't trust our friend who knows our hearts, secrets, flaws, fears etc., then that person stops being a friend, and becomes a lover for sex. After a while, we start using each other.
2. A chance to get a good vibe and connection before we think about committing to them.
3. The relationship is based on personal compatibility, not just sexual chemistry. And in a relationship where a friendship is the basis of the relationship, each person is free to love the other without the physical relationship being the main focus.
4. A meaningful, concrete friendship brings little fear of rejection.
5. We build solid foundations to grow from and to return to during hard times.
6. No hidden agendas.
7. We can learn each other's love language.

1. The vibe/chemistry/Spark/Lust/Fling is so strong that it feels like we've known them for years already. It seems like everything just clicks from the very start. In reality, we don't really know the person, but we are so caught up in "OMG I have a new bae" mode that we don't pay attention to the growing wildfire... "Sparks" fly.

2. **Feelings**: it's way easier to be friends with someone you're not attracted to. The only real distinction between friend and boy/girlfriend is the attraction and emotion factors. If I'm attracted to a woman, then it would be really difficult to want to only befriend her. I'll be "friendly," but I have deeper feelings: attraction; arousal.

3. **Horny**: you don't want to be friends. You just want to have sex and chill because you don't have time for a relationship and you're working on yourself... yeah, we know.

In conclusion, even if you skip being friends, you still have a chance to build one while together because there is always more to learn about someone. Being friends first simply means to reserve some "committed relationship behavior" for the actual relationship... if the feelings grow.

Don't let the Sparks blind you.

I AM THE LOVE OF MY LIFE

Dear Worth,

Dear self, don't lose yourself in your search for
acceptance by others. Be who you want to be, not
what others want to see. Prove yourself to
yourself, not others. The people worth
impressing want you to be yourself anyways.

You must think that they don't see the value in you. They DO!!!! It's way too obvious. I mean, you're faithful, loyal, honest, trustworthy, supportive, you have your own shit together and much more. You're telling me that they don't see your worth? REALLY? Get the fuck out of here...

What else do you have to do to show them you're good enough? News flash, they ALREADY see your qualities, **they just don't want you in the way that you want to be wanted**. That's the cold truth. If they wanted you in that certain way, they would show you. You can spend years trying to prove something that someone AREADY knows... Think about that.

Here's a plot twist though... How much are you actually proving? How much do you actually value yourself?

The evidence shows that you claim to value yourself, yet you're trying to prove to someone who's not appreciating you, that you "deserve" better. This shines a light on the difference between thinking you deserve better vs merely desiring better. How can you deserve better if you do not choose better? I believe that you deserve what you choose, and in this case, you're

187

choosing to prove your worth to someone who doesn't value you and to someone who already knows your worth but still doesn't want you!!! If you deserve better, prove it.

And that's why I say, if you truly value yourself, you wouldn't have to prove anything. In cases where you aren't being appreciated after giving it an honest try to work things out, leaving shows that you deserve better. How? Because you're taking your worth away from someone who does not appreciate it.

You desire better; you choose better; then you deserve better because you chose better, and earned it by leaving. I hope you understand what I'm saying. The point is, it's sad, but in a lot of cases, if you really want to prove your worth, you have to take it somewhere else before you lose it.

You will find yourself when you stop obsessively proving your worth to someone else. A man or woman should be with you because they value and appreciate who you are. Some people just want to let you constantly try to sell yourself to them because you over give to them and they reap the benefits without actually having to put in any effort since you overcompensate for their lack of effort. You want to prove your worth. So you cook more, you do more favors for them, you sacrifice more and right when you want them to reciprocate, they use the greatest excuses of all time "I'm not ready for relationship, I'm too busy, I'm damaged, my ex is crazy."

Because they know as soon as they give you what you've been working so hard for, they would have to keep doing it. And the whole point of not reciprocating in the first place is because they simply didn't want to keep doing it.

You don't need a standing ovation from anyone. You are enough right now. You have nothing to prove to anyone but yourself. Care less about who you are to others and more about who you are to yourself. You will have less heartaches and disappointments the minute you stop seeking from others the validation only YOU can give yourself.

The Victim Card

Insecure control freaks love to play the victim. They have discovered that when they are somebody's victim, they actually have a little bit of power over the person who "hurt them". If they are victims, they can manipulate the person who hurt them by making that person feel guilty and as if they "owe them something" or by draining their sympathy and attention. When they see how much it actually works, (they guilt trip you into staying) they then want to remain victims because of what they are getting out of the role. They put the responsibility for happiness on someone else because they themselves are not up for the task of making themselves happy. That way, anytime they are unhappy, it's never their fault. They rather blame someone else for their lack of happiness.

You may not realize this but just in case you don't, I'll fill you in. When you play the victim, you are actually making victims of the people you're using to make yourself feel better. Therefore, the person playing the victim is often the worst bullshitter. By intentionally making others feel guilty for hurting you, you then become a manipulative bully.

When you waste energy being bitter towards someone, you're wasting energy you could use to be happy.

190

Soul Mates

Do you believe in soul-mates?

What if the idea of soulmates is a myth? You meet that "right" person, fall in love, and ride off into the sunset happy forever. Sounds like a fairy tale? Love doesn't seem to work that way. Even in the best marriages I assume, love takes a lot of work. The idea of all of us having soulmates seems romantic to plenty of people, but obsessing over the "one true soul mate" concept appears to be more destructive than romantic in my eyes. It's a nice thought, on the surface, but with some implications, if you think about it.

What happens if you marry someone who you thought was your soulmate, and then your real soulmate comes along? Do you ditch your current relationship, and it's totally justifiable? "Bad news, see what happened was, I can't help it, that's my SOUL MATE!" What happens when we don't end up with our one soul mate? Are we then destined for unhappiness, while those who find their soul mates are significantly happier? And what happens if you think you've found your soul mate, then you have an argument? Or you go through rough times? Do you decide that since things are so hard this ***can't*** be your soul mate, so you'd better opt out of the relationship and keep looking? Think about how many times we found someone and thought that they were our soulmates, but they turned out not to be.

191

I AM THE LOVE OF MY LIFE

I have struggled with this belief of one woman being my only one soul mate. Life has taught me that every time I thought I had found my one soulmate, it was just a "soul tie" with sex. I realized that while the idea of a soulmate keeps us hopeful, it can also be misleading and blinding.

I believe that there are a lot people out there that are compatible with me/you/others. The issue is that we don't really know how to find them because we try to force the compatibility with people who don't truly fit us. Forcing shit is not romantic at all.

Just think about how unromantic the idea of having one predetermined soulmate could be. The idea that you "*have*" to end up with that one person does not always sound romantic. Some people see it as it's romantic to have one destined soul mate and to battle through life to finally run into that one person, and recognize each other's hearts while spilling drinks on a train. On the other hand, I personally believe that the idea that you have many potential soulmates, but would choose each & every day to be committed to one seems much more romantic to me. What do you think?

After realizing this, I now do not believe that there is ONE set soul mate for anyone. I believe in multiple soul mates in the form of family, lovers and friends. I think the idea of one set soul-mate for romance is nearly destructive because it sets up improbable expectations with reality. The universe does not have just one fixed soul for your soul. It has many souls.

The universe contains many souls mates; some that match better with you and some who do not. So, out of the 7 billion people, you'll find many that compliment your personality, others who do not. If you miss one, you'll run into another, but to do that you have to believe that there are more than one out there. The one you choose to settle with becomes your mate for life, because you both **chose** *to be with one soul.*

With that being said, I see no perfect matches; I see lots of good and great matches and we will find at least one sooner or later.

The bad side of the truth about soulmates that people don't tell us: It could keep weak minded people in check. It makes hopeless romantics hang in there and put up with bullshit relationships and not open their eyes to the reality of situations because they have faith that it will get better. We even pray about God changing our "soul mate" to treat us better. It makes us stay with cheaters because, "they are our soul mates". It makes people who are just at the dating stage agree to being exclusive, but not committed, because "we are soul mates".

Dear Faith

God gave the other person free will. Therefore, *you* can pray about the relationship all you want, but how is that going to help when the other person is working against your faith by CHOICE? When the other person is CHOOSING to do things that destroy relationships? If they have free will, God won't MAKE them act right because they aren't CHOOSING to act right on their own. It is currently not in their heart. THEY have to want it. Your faith strengthens YOU because you choose to believe and work on YOU. When it comes to a relationship, both people need to submit to the same faith.

is that your
soul mate or
your distraction?

Soul Ties

When you are in a sexual relationship with someone, and you allow them to mistreat you, use you and insult you, yet you find it difficult to opt out of the relationship, and you stay because the sex is amazing.... you may have a soul tie, not love. Your soul is infected.

I'm not affiliated with any particular religion. I'm simply a believer in a higher power and energy. I believe in soul ties. They've hunted me for a while until just recently. I thought that I was having emotionless sex, but was actually tying my soul, exchanging energies, with women who were spiritually infected. They had STDS, but not the kind that burn or itch – they had **Sexually Transmitted DEMONS.**

I KNEW they were broken from past relationships and I still went forward with sex because it felt good. It blew me away every time. Of course, I ignored the bad vibes I got from these women. Therefore, the more I ignored it, the worse vibes I felt growing within.

Little did I know, I was inheriting their pain, drama, vibes, insecure energy, and pieces of their souls. Why was it so easy for my male friends to run after sex at every corner, but when I did it, I felt emptier inside?

The last girl was the last straw. I'm there, having sex, after a conversation about how much her ex used to beat

195

on her; how no guy had ever actually made her the main chick; how she always played the side chick role... she felt like she was never enough, she never took the time to heal, she was constantly manipulated, used by men and was looking for HELP, not my love.

She was accustomed to settling for less. And all of a sudden, I was less. I was settling for less. I was inheriting her "less". She didn't want love, she wanted help. Why was I there? Why did I keep going back? I KNEW she was no good for me at the time because she had become just as manipulative as her exes... but I kept going back. I knew that we didn't have a good chance at a happy future and I still ran back to her bed. I literally felt addicted... like my demons fell in love with her demons.

My discovery: sexual intercourse is more than a fun experience. It involves a unity of souls. Some people have sex to release frustration or just for fun. But sex is more than that.

Every time you have sex with someone, you become one flesh with that person. You are united with that person in every way. Your spirit, emotions, every aspect of your being is combined with that person. Imagine fusing your soul with multiple broken people...

The Unties

We may have an addiction to the demon and drama of the other person. Therefore, we may need an addiction to get over another one. This may sound foolish, but what if we need another engaging obsession (possibly a self-motivated and healthy one) to get over our previous obsessiveness? I, for instance, post on social media. Whenever I feel like being expressive, I write and it has turned out to be the most productive and engaging addictions I've had. Instead of ruining my soul with exes, I WRITE.

So, pick up another habit, not alcohol or a new rebound relationship, but something that you'll be proud of later. Turn over a new leaf and let your soul heal and cleanse. Let's try not to detach from our feelings and pay careful attention to our attachments and let them go if they do not serve us well.

Remedy: Exercise and meditation/prayer are some of the best treatments for everything from depression, anxiety to an empty soul. Exercise is not a cure-all, but it helps cure many things in life. Give it a shot.

*Some people are stuck
to each other only because
their demons are in love
with each other*

You ruin each other every time.
You want to be free, but you
want each other to be miserable
if you're not together. You
manipulate each other. You
distract each other. You
diss each other. You stalk
each other. You prey on each
other's insecurities...

**Your demons are still in love with
each other.**

It goes way beyond physical, you have
spiritual bonding...

SELF

The greatest hindrance is not accepting myself as my one true love. Logically, I know that within myself I have all the tools. But honestly, I do not ALWAYS feel that. I often feel that I need something outside of me to witness my love.

Why is that?

Whenever someone tells me about how they are looking for love or how so and so doesn't treat them the way they want to be treated, I always ask them if they have looked in the mirror and loved themselves the way they require others to love them. I ask them, how can you love anyone if you don't at least try to love yourself? Too many of us walk around expecting love from others, but never try to love the one person who is most important. **SELF.**

What if we took that term, soul mate, and looked at a mirror? Maybe we would see that a soul mate is not always someone else; it does not have to be outside of me. It could be the assembly of my soul and self within. We end up using valuable time dismissing the opportunities to accept and love ourselves.

Are you looking for the ONE? Stop. You are the one. **You are the love of your life.**

Your soulmate doesn't have to be someone else who you ATTRACT, it could be YOU. Your soulmate is simply an expression of your Self. As you connect more with your own soul, that another soul will come to you as a mirrored manifestation of who and what you are. It is not always about finding your soulmate outside of you, but removing the barriers so you can find peace within.

BE your own SOULMATE too

Fuckboyism

Fuckboyism: The tendency to hide insecurities while utilizing mendacious and manipulative tactics to get what they want from people in order to feel "happy" or at least satisfied, while not truly caring about the wellbeing of the other person... personal satisfaction is all at the expense of someone else's emotional and mental stability. In a nutshell, what our generation calls **fuckboys** and **fuckgirls** are viewed as insecure narcissists. They are extremely charming and convincing emotional con artists, they make you feel guilty most of the time and in order for their games to work, they have to come across naïve, gullible, damaged and hurt people who do not know the signs. They prey on the weak and deceive the strong.

What is a "Fuckboy"

They're most often wolves in sheep's clothing. I'm talking about a very specific type of man **and woman** and their behavior. This "I don't mind fucking you over to get what I want" mindset is a very common thought pattern that I have observed. A Fuckboy or girl aka Master Manipulators are very insecure people who choose not to be mature and "real", hide behind ego, pride and lies while using manipulation tactics to make themselves seem more impressive than who they REALLY are. They seem to be the ideal **woman or man** following the **womanly/gentlemanly** rules, going out with you for

201

dinner, enthusiastic about you, interested in your life and listen to you attentively. They are probably very attractive, good talkers, fun to hang out with, and seem to be great candidates for relationships. They demonstrate great promise and potential. They will be so seemingly genuinely into you, they'll say that they want to be exclusive and not date other people. And you can't understand why sex with them drives you crazy. Then they fuck you over inside and out.

Full Anatomy of Fuckboyism

Liars - This is the easiest thing to pick up on because the more you get to know a person, the more you see that things don't add up. They try to deceive you and lie to make you believe that they have a real connection with you or want an exclusive relationship with you while actually only desiring sex, financial gain, popularity, or attention and acceptance. They are compulsive liars because it affects every part of their lives in order to hide their cheating from you and whoever else may snitch. They even lie to themselves. The irony is that they never own up to lies, they just pile more on top, and then fail to understand why they can't dig themselves out. Lying results in them getting what they want more often than when they tell the truth. They KNOW that you prefer the truth, but imagine someone telling you that they want to be with you, your best friend... and later a few random people around town.... You would most likely reject and maybe even leave them. So, they choose to lie so that they can have the best of both worlds.

They are frauds that pretend to be strong, pretend to be the realest to ever live, yet as soon as you step to them, they wine and manipulate their way out of the heat. You find that most of the things about them that initially caught your interest were lies, wisely orchestrated to deceive you and betray your trust just because they wanted bits and pieces of you, not the whole thing.

Flirts – they flirt with everyone even when it clearly makes you feel uncomfortable because they love attention and are enthusiastic attention-seekers. For example, commenting on other people's pictures with roses, hearts and heart-eye emojis. This type of behavior is often used to jump start chemistry with other people which has the potential to evolve into cheating. They flirt in person and on social media almost religiously.

Commitment Issues – they are often afraid of the idea of commitment because of its risks. They feel that the heartache of trying to be great for one person but ending up getting played isn't worth the risk of commitment anymore and prefers to spend their time validating themselves with the acceptance of person after person after person. Instead of committing to one person, they commit to trying to get "more hoes".

Emotional – they need constant validation and acceptance from people so that they can believe that they are valued. They have a void to fill that having one

203

partner can't. They are actually afraid of being alone. The fear they have of being alone might make them pursue multiple people to mess around with as added attention, entertainment and security. But they do not want anyone to leave them and that's why they leave first or act up when you try to move on with someone else. They catch and lose feelings on a consistent basis. They cry. They are very dramatic. They get mad over the smallest things.

They can't communicate properly because they are so defensive and passive aggressive and blow up when they can no longer hold things in. They don't know how to let things go after getting caught or exposed so they argue their point until you give up after being called "crazy". They even send long ass emotionally driven text messages full of all of the bullshit that they hold inside, like "we aren't even together, Oh, so you calling me a liar?" and as soon as you start hitting them with FACTS and PROOF they STILL try to run around the questions or run from the "relationship" when playing the emotionally abused victim card doesn't work.

They are sooooo emotional but act like they don't care. They care but they are using their "I'm hurt and broken, no one understands me" act to get you to megatron-transform into Mrs. or Mr. "save-a-hoe", all ready to repair the victim and save THEIR day. It's clearly a cry for attention that we are too blind to see. So, when we get tired of it, we step to them but they hit us with "This is why I don't get close to anyone. This is why I don't do relationships." Now we feel like we're on a verge of a break up and regret saying anything in the first place.

Greedy – Some people are never satisfied emotionally, sexually, or mentally and are constantly looking for new and more fulfillment from multiple people. It is not possible to fulfill the desires of a greedy person because THEY don't even know how to satisfy themselves fully. They feel satisfied for the moment but don't want to commit to developing any long term satisfaction because it requires the amount of effort that they just don't want to give. They want cake and to eat it too.

Jealous – jealousy is their way of reflecting on their own unfaithfulness so they will often accuse you of doing the same thing they're doing, even when you are completely innocent. They love being single while getting relationship benefits without having to actually be in a relationship. But, they want you to be their "just in case bae". The "just in case bae" is the person who is seemingly marriage material "just in case" they are ever ready to settle down. They don't want anyone else to have you even when **they** won't have you. They want you to wait for them to finish fucking around. So, they hate when someone else makes you happy because they know that they are incapable of making you THAT happy consistently. They need the bar to stay low.

Manipulative narcissist – While they seem great at first, these **men and women** display sneaky narcissistic and sketchy, selfish behaviors. They feel entitled to whatever they can take from you. They will exploit all of you and even those close to you for their own needs and pleasures. They are selfish and greedy. They confuse you better to be able to use you better.

They attempt to abuse your mind. They psychologically manipulate you in order to keep their fuckery hidden. For example, they call you crazy so that you will stop focusing on their sneaky shit, and instead make you think that your logic is the issue.

Being manipulative is an art that most of them practice because they know that if they don't perfect the deception, they'll get caught up.

Manipulator Mindset

Let's say they KNOW:
- you love them,
- you worry about them,
- you feel the need to prove your worth to them,
- you are afraid to tell them how you REALLY feel,
- you are often naive,
- you are very sensitive and soft hearted.

But, they take all these things and use them against you to get something they want which doesn't benefit YOU at all. That is manipulation. If they didn't stop but instead started doing it with everyone else they dated, they set off on a path of destruction.

Men and women who are players eventually realize the trail of broken hearts that they leave behind. It's innate to look for meaning in all things, and after a while they all become aware, bored or lonely enough, and perhaps they might ask themselves "why am I still doing this? Why am I playing so many games?" There are several explanations: boredom, anger with the opposite gender, or it could just be a psychological issue and bad habit or pleasure.

I've been around men and women who play each other. Most of my college football team, groups of close friends, and plenty of the cheerleaders and sorority girls were called fuckboys and hoes. They're good friends to me, but sometimes they just don't know what damage they're causing in each other's lives. I've seen them "toot and boot" each other religiously. I know that's pretty evil, but I've seen it. They're not the same type of manipulator, they are very different with the games that they play; different mindsets.

People have lost all respect for relationships these days. I have a friend who claims to love his wife. I've started to notice that he truly feels as though he does. However, every time he goes out, he will pick up other women effortlessly. He will tell them up front that he has a wife (other guys won't tell), but women **still** hand over their numbers... so fuckboyism isn't only a guy problem, it's a willing side chick problem too. Some of these women are way too messy and do not give a damn about a man having a girlfriend or a wife as long as they get their piece of him.

Side Chicks Level 99

They are only looking for dick, attention and if you want to drop a few hundred dollars on the rent or give them paid vacations with their Instagram famous friends, they'll keep their mouths closed until they catch stronger feelings. Some of these women are insecure and feel like they cannot get their own men so they accept half of someone else's. Some women look for love in any form they can get it because they have not received the love they needed in the past. Think about it, a man who already has a girlfriend or wife but treating his side chick well, and at least tells her the truth is better, in her eyes, than the single men who she has had before him.

Side chicks who know that they are side chicks think that if they try hard enough, this man will love them as much as they love their girlfriend and even living with that lie is good enough for them. The man's main chick may be happy... because she doesn't know what's going on. The side chick wants to have **that** happiness with **that** man, not another man.

So, please don't think this epidemic of players is all on **men**... they cheat with **women** who are willing to help men cheat for their own benefits. The side piece effect.

Hidden Guilt

You may be wondering, how do players keep their conscience clear and guilt free? I think it's more about their perspective and how they see the world and the opposite sex, which helps hide the guilt feeling. They see that there are already plenty of people getting cheated on right now. They see so many women having meaningless sex and how other men are doing the same. They observe how plenty of people aren't following the traditional methods of dating. So, it's simple, they consider dating in itself as already fucked up. An example would be: If dating was a riot, the manipulative woman or man would consider themselves to be just another thief looking free shit to take. They look around and notice that they aren't the only ones doing wrong; not the only ones with fuckery methods. Every single person they get just adds to their deteriorating morality. They see everyone as dirty. It's all a matter of perspective.

How To Avoid A Fuckboy/Fuckgirl

There are more Fuck Boys/Girls than ever in this world full of red flags but we choose to ignore the signs. To even make it to the point where we have sex, demonstrates that we didn't take the time to uncover their fuckery and true character. Then to continue ignoring signs until we make it to a relationship, shows that we were attracted to the insecurities in them because it matches up with the insecurities within ourselves. Then to constantly chase them after seeing for ourselves who they REALLY are shows that we choose to save them more than we want to save ourselves. Thus, we will keep ending up with these types of people until we learn to listen to our intuition.

Our gut will be right more times than it will be wrong. When someone is more interested in pleasing themselves than pleasing us even when it's at the expense of our wellbeing, it should be obvious that we are being repeatedly fucked over. Our gut is that internal, unconscious voice that warns us to fall back. Start noticing what your body does when you feel uncomfortable with someone's behavior. Do you start to feel depleted like your energy has been sucked out of your body? If so, opt out!

See, it's one thing wanting to find your Mr. or Mrs.

210

Right but it's another to be able to identify them. Your biggest challenge won't be finding the right person for the moment because the right person for the moment could literally be anywhere and anyone at any time. Your biggest challenge will be recognizing a "good person" who can fulfil your needs in the right way for more than just a moment. The thing is, we can meet a great person for that moment, and when the moment is over, the rest of the time dealing with them consists of us trying to either change them back to who they first showed us they were, or into who we think they have the potential to be.

Most of these Situationships with **fuckboys and girls** could be avoided if we know how to distinguish a good short term partner from a good long term partner from the BEGINNING stages. I want you to take this section of the book seriously because it's often a mistake if we leave it all to chance like "let's just see what happens" because we're worthy of the love that we **seek**, not just in the short-term but also in the long-term.

Learn the Red Flags. We should give our relationships time to grow slowly so we can see if any red flags surface. And have solid boundaries. It's important that our boundaries are strong enough so that if someone does violate our standards, we can quickly redefine their role in our lives. While "they all seem good at first," most fuckboys/girls have several personality traits that distinguish them from other people. The traits can range from being tremendously flirtatious to compulsively lying.

The better you can identify the personality traits and red flags of a fuckboy/girl, the better chance of not ending up with one.

Stay A Good Guy

Quality guys who avoid the "fuckboy" mentality are rare these days and usually there is a stereotype placed on them saying that they finish last. A lot of people these days think that women see Mr. good guy as desperate and boring simps; that good guys usually get overwhelmed with infatuation because they seem to be all into love and relationships more than the "average" guy. People also seem to believe that these type of guys are usually the first in the friend zone because their super-gentleman, "yes man" behavior actually worked against them, in a way, for being "too nice."

But, the truth is, all women love good, friendly gentlemen. However, they may not always want to date them simply because being nice is the only thing some of those men bring to the certain women's tables, thinking that they should be rewarded for "niceness" and entitled to sex. No, bro, being nice doesn't grant you all access to women. You need to be more than a nice guy.

If you are a good guy, stay a good guy. Good guys are dope and unique; Peaceful; Respectful; Honest. You do not need to tap into your inner fuckboyiotic-gene in order to get the women you want just because you perceive jerks as "winning". I know that it may seem like women crave "jerks" but I'm convinced that the excitement, challenges, and adventures that come along with "jerks" are what's keeping those women's panties wet. This makes sense. Why else would most women choose to

213

stay with men who are considered "jerks"? There must be some attractive traits that are eye-catching to women in which those "jerks" possess that you may not have discovered within yourself yet, and it's not their lies, not their disrespect or cheating that's keeping women there. It's the confidence, creativity, excitement, a woman's hope and view of those "jerk's" "potential".

Stay a good man. The few things that you will always have over men who manipulate women are genuine love and peaceful love for women and not just a craving for sex and control. When you compare years of experience being a good man versus years of being a **fuckboy**, you have years of knowing how to treat women respectfully... But a **fuckboy** has years of experience manipulating women and PRETENDING to care. This is a habit that will continue until he realizes he can never fully accept himself while he continues to mistreat people and steal value from others. Unfortunately, his lifestyle is very fun in the short-term and it's hard to grow out of this mindset. It's only after long-term dissatisfaction that he'll begin to change.

All you need is to stay a good man, but find ways to empower yourself with good sex skills, creativity, edge, more confidence, firmness, ambition, security, the ability to stand up for yourself, the ability to say **no** and mean it and have some swag. At the end, if a fuckboy ever wants to settle down with a woman, he has to learn the gentlemanly traits that you have already been sharpening throughout your whole life.

214

Being a good man is always best. It works in your favor later with the right woman for you; when she is deciding if whether or not you are a keeper. Everyone wants to build something with a good person.

A Man Who Is Afraid To Love

What about the man who is "afraid" to love? No one sits him down and gives him speeches about how he's supposed to be and how to embrace his emotions like they do for women. The message men get is that "Emotions are for women" and to maintain control at all costs without being vulnerable or weak.

Well, love has this amazing ability to make you feel out of control, vulnerable and sometimes weak, other times strong. So, it conflicts with the male programming. One of the main reasons why I think men are "afraid of love" is due to fear of getting played and laughed at for seeming too "soft." The man who is always in his feelings about women hurting him appears weak. So, they often say, "that's why you need to stop saving these hoes" or "that's why you need to stop trying to settle with these women and have fun while you can." They pick on him and make it worse, actually.

I know this by personal experience. I was that guy; I have friends who are **THAT** guy now. I learned that Love and fear are opposites. How can I find what I'm afraid to embrace? It's scary because nobody can control it. When you've got it, you're stuck with it. LOVE...

I have learned that men fear love because men aren't given the knowledge or insight on how to embrace emotions... Women on the other hand, are taught how to embrace emotions. Women have no problem discussing

216

their feelings with each other, and are given the benefit of the experiences of those other women who are older and wiser. Men don't always have the benefit of those experiences from older men, because a lot of older men these days are still hitting clubs "getting money and fucking bitches"; still telling us not to settle; still telling us that it's not about love, it's about sex and money.

He might be "afraid to love" because no one has ever fully caught **him**, but he's afraid to even attempt to catch just one woman and hold her tightly enough so he won't feel the need to seek other women because he just doesn't know how, or may not have that desire. On top of that, the Bachelor life often times seems more interesting than settling down with one woman when he notices that there are plenty of women out there embracing **"Hoe Is Life."**

This doesn't mean that women need to go out teaching men to love them. This means that men need to find out how to embrace love for themselves before they damage more women. It means that men need to also teach each other how to be masculine while embracing their emotions. Let us learn our lessons. Let us evolve. Don't be the woman who thinks she is being loyal just because she sticks around after we constantly disrespect and cheats on her. Don't be the "Mrs. fix it" woman who thinks she can stop a man from being a liar and manipulator. Don't be the woman who sticks around and defend us when everyone else sees our consistent bullshit. You need to save yourself, not us.

217

Sticking around to be repeatedly fucked over is not loyalty, that's called being an enabler. You are not helping us heal, you are choosing to be on the receiving end of our bullshit. We won't see a flaw in our ways if you make it acceptable and act like it is tolerable just because you "love us and are loyal."

Let us go so that we can see that we need to grow. Not only for your own good, but for ours as well. Even when we KNOW our behavior is often morally wrong (lying, using, cheating, and mentally, emotionally, physically abusive), we will continue to do it if you continue to put up with it. There is no better way to prove that you deserve better than walking away and SHOWING it.

When you walk away, you show a man that his behavior is not only unacceptable to you, but that it is unacceptable for other women as well and is also damaging to his own character. A man can be sooooo used to being a fuck up that he starts believing that its ok to be that way; that there are no issues within. When you walk away, he actually has time to focus on his own inner chaos. Your enabling nature is no longer distracting him from recognizing his own demons. Don't you see, that as long as you stick around as a placeholder and as an enabler, you become one of his demons!! He controls **your** chaos.

Don't break your own rules.

218

Don't go back on your own word and run back to him once you see that instead of working on his character, he chose to find a new woman to fuck with. Let him. Over time, he will learn. Let him. It is HIS lesson to learn and not yours to teach.

What happens when he still chooses to be a user and abuser, is that it becomes so ingrained in his day to day life that it affects his perspective of women. He won't see any as "enough for him" because they keep leaving. They keep complaining about who he really is. They won't put up with him. He stops trusting them because no woman sticks around to tolerate him anymore. His games are getting old. The fuckboy ways are old and instead of seeing him as "potential" they start to see him as a lame. If it is so easy for him to lie, he thinks it is just as easy for women to lie. If it is so easy for him to cheat or to get other women to cheat, he thinks a woman would do him the same way... he is afraid of karma!

Even a man who constantly hurts others does not want a taste of his own medicine. As soon as you give them a dose of the bullshit that they've been giving you, they cry about YOU poisoning them. It's crazy because instead of seeing his behavior as the issue, he claims that women are the issue: "These hoes ain't loyal", but fail to realize that no woman wants to put up with the bullshit forever.

Look, if a man wants to grow, he will choose a path and commit to it. This goes for if he wants to be a better man and even if he wants to be a better cheater. Let him. If he wants to grow, let him go and then you'll know. If you let go, let go with a sense of it being the final straw and there is no way you'll take him back. Don't be the girl who "fake break up" just to see if he'll chase you. It'll always backfire; that's the "enabler" mindset. If he is afraid to love you, let him go. let him go. let him go. let him go. let him go. let him go. let him go. let him go. let him go. let him go. let him go. let him go.

Put her in her place

I believe that a man should always treat a woman with respect but he has to be able to let her know when she has him fucked all the way up... **respectfully**. Put her in her place **RESPECTFULLY!** He has to have the balls to tell a woman when her wishes are unrealistic or unfair. And be willing to cut her ass off regardless of how cute or sexy she is to him. If we come to understand that attractive, respectful, professional, honest, great dick skilled, and trustworthy men are way harder to come by than a sexy woman, it will give us a higher level of confidence when pursuing women. Of course we want to make her happy but we can't let these women walk all over us and fear losing them so much that we allow ourselves to be taken advantage of. We can make genuine changes for ourselves that we feel will make **us** happy, and that won't just make a woman happy because at end of the day, we still want to be love for being ourselves, right?

I AM THE LOVE OF MY LIFE

fake tough

I'm tired of being fake tough or pretending like I'm not "in my feelings." If you asked me, being in my feelings is force myself to be emotionally unavailable because I'll keep hurting people and attracting people who are just like me: emotionally unavailable. I connect through emotions, not just physical contact and proximity. That's why I now embrace who I am. If I don't, I'll feel like I'm the problem. I'll always feel like I'm not enough. I'll always feel like I have to change a lot about myself to seem more compatible. What I want is to be myself and someone can love me for that. If I'm someone who's in touch with emotions, I don't want to fake like I'm always tough, just because I think I'll end up in the friend zone for being "too emotional." Fuck that. I'm me.

Being fake just to appeal to people makes you a D-Level fuckboy these days, even when your intentions are to claim her and be with her. Why? Because even though your intentions are semi-good, you're still not being yourself. That means, if she gives in, she's giving an opportunity to the fake version of you. Therefore, in order to keep her satisfied, you have to keep up with that fake version. Over time, you'll get exhausted and you eventually turn back into who you really are. And she'll see you for the liar and pretender you are.

Dear Future Wife,

"My love, I will be attracted to other women. They may briefly cross my mind, but don't panic. I only want you. I will notice them. I will see them in stores and at work. I will hold doors open for them and smile. I will offer to help them lift big objects. I will give up my seat for them when there are no seats left. I will notice them at the park. I will notice them on TV and in movies. I will see them at bars when I'm out with the fellas. Some of them will be attracted to me as well. But, I promise to choose YOU each and every time and I promise to never let any thoughts and urges get the best of me. I promise to fight compulsions and to always be respectful. This means, out of all the attractive women in the world who I notice, I want you to know that I see THEM, but I only want YOU. I crave you. I choose you for more than physical attraction. I choose you because of spiritual bonding. My soul yearns for your soul, only. They may catch my eyes every now and then but you caught my heart! And I promise to protect what we have, all ways, always."

Horacio Jones

I AM THE LOVE OF MY LIFE

Hunters, Fanciers And Gatherers

Talking about gender is such a touchy subject. See, my opinion is that not all men are hunters, and the implication that women are prey makes me uncomfortable, to be honest. The stereotyped assumption and attitudes about how all men should ALWAYS be the ones to pursue breeds gender inequality! I believe that if a man can seek a wife, a woman can seek a husband.

I am sure some men want to hunt, and some women like to be chased. As long as they find each other, that's okay. But, you, as a man, do not have to **act** a certain way in the dating game. Do what comes natural to you, and you should attract women who will respond in kind. If you aren't a "hunter", your life still has immense value.

Most of us are only aware of obvious physical, biological or behavioral attributes that differ between genders. Science of course shows that most men are hunters, most women want to be hunted; most men want to be the powerhouse and most women want to be the soft spots; things such as competing and winning are what most men thrive on; women by nature desire attention.

However, some of the guys I know do not always align with being hunters. They consider it old school and so do some of their girlfriends and wives. It's old school. It gives men a bad name; makes us all look like savages who

SHOULD always chase and court women first or else we "lack confidence or don't really want her because he didn't act first." Men have a hard time trying to detach themselves from this stereotype.

Now, I am no way saying that men should be like "prey"; waiting for a woman to find him, take him out on a date, pay for his meals and walk him to his door. No, that is not what I am saying. What I mean is that women can be more upfront about who they want. A man who wants her back will not let her do all of the work.

Of course some men still "hunt". And there are women who prefer that type of man. But that does not have to impact **you**. Bro, Be shy. Have good manners. Be a gentleman. Treat women respectfully. Learn how they differ from us, and how fascinating their differences are. If you really take the time to listen to them, observe them as beautiful beings, no one will ever look at you as "thirsty", "hunter" or call you weak just because you're a fancier; a man who like women to be more upfront and inviting so that he can meet her half way. You'll be a sincere, humble man who will interest other women because you're different in a very likable way instead of trying to pursue women the way that most men are told they HAVE to.

There is nothing wrong if you don't place yourself in the role of a "hunter". We live in a society where finding partners for companionship is exaggerated as a cat and mouse game and that you can get who you want if only you play by the specific rules.

The truth is, there are three types of men in this world: the hunters, gatherers and the fanciers. And, the sooner you can figure out which one a man is, the easier it will be to figure out what type of guy aligns with you the best. And if you are a man, knowing that you will be accepted by the woman you deserve, if only you stay true to who you are, should be a confidence booster.

Communication

The hunter uses more actions than words.
The fancier us more words than actions.
The gatherer says the right thing, but his words are devoid of meaning because he never backs them up.

Self-reliance

The hunter is most confident.
The fancier is humbly self-assured.
The gatherer is driven by insecurity.

External Swaying

The hunter stands on his own two feet.
The fancier stands on his circle of friends and family. He supports himself and also looks to others for advice, motivation and care.
The gatherer looks for people to feed off of and makes victims out of everyone so that his life doesn't seem as

bad from the outside looking in.

Openness

The hunter is frank about his intentions, subtle about feelings, and acts on both of them without the fear of rejection.

The fancier is honest about his feelings with a woman and embraces them, while subtle with intentions.

The gatherer hides his true feelings and fears rejection.

Power

The hunter is assertive. He makes the plans. He takes majority of the control. He makes the final decisions. Most things need to go his way. He wants the majority of the power in the relationship.

The fancier understands an equal amount of effort is required from both the man and the woman for a relationship to flourish.

The gatherer would rather lose a woman than risk not having "the upper hand" in a relationship. Or he would let her think she has the upper hand because he doesn't have to do anything; she'll take care of it.

Manipulation

The hunter pursues a woman by being upfront, direct and blunt about wanting to be intimate.

The fancier pursues a woman in terms of friendship

initiation, building, and nurturing... before trying to convert the friendship to a relationship.

The gatherer gives a little of himself, but expects a lot in return. He wants to be a woman's whole world, but only wants her to be a piece of his. He is a taker, not a giver.

Self-confidence

The hunter knows who he is and doesn't care about superficial attention. He looks to his woman for mostly respect and appreciation.

The fancier looks to his woman for mostly reciprocity, equality, appreciation, reassurance, and encouragement.

The gatherer looks to his woman for validation.

Trustworthiness

The hunter is bluntly honest with you.

The fancier often softens the blow with his honesty.

The gatherer would rather lie than have to deal with the consequences of the truth.

Protection

The hunter defends you. He would never let anyone talk shit about you in public or private.

The fancier secures you. He'll look for safer ways to handle people who disrespects you without having to risk your or his own life in the process.

The gatherer will let others disrespect you because he

does it all the time. He'll rather let you look crazy.

Safekeeping

The hunter and fancier physically works toward creating a future with you. The hunter may not be able to express it with words, but he will show it with his action. The fancier shows consistency between words and actions. The gatherer works on creating a future with you through his words only. Rarely backs up anything.

The Cons

Hunters – usually cocky, over aggressive and bluntly honest with you, even if it's something you don't want to hear. When it comes to confrontations with other disrespectful men, they rather fight before talking it out. They are sometimes emotionally unavailable and say "you know I'm bad at expressing myself." They often have trouble with pride and ego.

Fanciers – they start off by trying to be friends first and sometimes get stuck in the friend zone because they wait too long to "make a move." They grow into emotionally available Hunters.

Gatherers – usually **fuckboys**. Fear rejection, and that's why he manipulates her with the victim card. They seek validation, even if that means it is at the expense of her feelings. Gatherers are more likely to allow her name to be brought up in a negative context without defending

230

her at all. He wants her to feel guilty for rejecting him because it might make her stay. He gives just enough of himself so that the woman would open up and give more of herself... he plays the give and take game.

Dear self,

Women are always told that if they show interest or anything first, men will become disinterested and chasing them will no longer be something they'll want to do. While this is true for some men, I have observed that this is far from the truth for most men.

If you intentionally make it hard for me to get to know you, eventually I'm going to let you go. I'm not going to chase anyone. Real men don't chase women who are obviously playing games and running away.

I read about advice that women give to one another saying to **never** initiate contact, ignore texts and respond to missed calls hours later, and not to show too much interest. If you don't do any of these, he will become disinterested because men's natural instinct is to chase/hunt something they feel is unattainable.

In other words, women are being told to play games (hard to get, make him beg)? Then those women turn around to complain about how men are not men enough to approach them and so on. Or that the men who DO approach them are **fuckboys**.

I truly consider myself as a good man and I would not waste my time with anyone who takes the advice those women have been given. I believe that dating is a delicate balancing act. Yes, I kinda like to pursue, but at the same time I have to get feedback that she's being receptive to

232

my approaches. And I also like being pursued as well. I don't mind going after a girl, it can be fun and it feels rewarding if I actually "get" her but I'm also really terrible at catching some of the subtle hints women can throw out letting you know they're ok with your advances. I honesty prefer more direct and assertive women.

We cannot ignore that the power and roles of men and women in relationships have changed. Nowadays, women are just as capable of wearing the "pants" in relationships as men. I call them alpha females. They love being in charge. They love the leadership roles. They are powerful, assertive women. Their confidence may be due to their good looks and/or superior intelligence and character.

Most men desire them, but men with huge egos and pride, and women with low self-esteem hates them. They are often intimidating and aren't afraid to go for who and what they want. They adjust to the new school dating scene where instead of waiting for men to approach them, they approach the men THEY want. They don't care about society telling them that they look desperate thirsty or needy. They don't care about the sayings "men are hunters; men go for who they want; a man who finds a wife" because they know that women are capable of hunting, going for who they want and finding a husband as well.

Dear Locked Doors,

when a woman likes us,
she will start opening her
doors all around her for us
to get to her. All we have to
do is walk through confidently,
creativity, honestly & respectfully.
Once we get inside, we can't
stop trying. There will be more
doors. Courting doesn't stop
once we "get her"

This is one of the most important dating tips to remember: No one wants to "chase" the other and that's perfectly ok. If she's interested, she'll open a door for you. Walk through. Not run! Don't be thirsty or too eager. Walk. Slowly, confidently, honestly, respectfully and creatively. The more interested she becomes, the more doors she opens. The more comfortable she is, the more doors she opens. The more she gets to know you and trust you... More doors open.

When you do those things, she will either open up more doors or start to close them. If she opens more doors, continue walking. Don't sprint... Remember, you're not chasing her. You are not thirsty. You are not desperate. Walk Honestly, respectfully, confidently, and creatively. More doors, more effort, more courting. No complacency.

When she's opening doors, she's also walking through towards you. She is also putting in effort. She's not running because she's not chasing you either. You are walking towards each other, opening doors. If you want each other, you WILL close the doors to your past and continue through the doors towards a future.

If doors start closing while you're being yourself, honest, respectful, creative, and confident.... Don't run!

There are plenty lessons to be learned and appropriated: 1st. Know when to walk away and when to take action. People are allowed to be uninterested in you. You don't have to start desperately proving your worth just to stop someone from losing interest. When doors close, don't try to run through, don't try to kick them open. Let them close. Why? Because they don't want you to come in. So let's not become obsessed with proving our worth. 2nd. Turn around while you still can... Or you'll end up "chasing" someone.

Captain Save A Hoe

So there's this woman. You've known her for a while, and you've always been interested in her. You both go to the same college or work together... or live in the same city... or you slid in her DM, got her number and "just getting to know her."

Every time you two talk, she keeps telling you stories about all these shitty guys she keeps dating. She talks about how she was cheated on. She talks about being damaged and having trust issues. She goes on and on about guys who manipulate and use her emotionally; guys who fuck her and then don't call her back.

Your natural reaction is probably going to feel like you need to fix her and protect her. You may have this intense urge to be her missing piece or to help her recover from whatever pain she's feeling. And you're thinking... If only she could see what it's like to date a great guy like you. You're going to want to rescue her. You're going to feel the craving to liberate her. You're going to want to release her pain and insecurities. You're going to want to save her.

In my **Bryson Tiller** Voice...   Don't

Don't save her. Watch out for women with poor decision making skills who allows their lives to swirl out of control with men. She needs self-love, not to love someone else. I KNOW that a broken, damaged woman with emotional baggage isn't your true idea of dating material. Let her heal for her before she deals with you.

I'll help people on their journey, but I never forget whose journey it is and I will not waste my time if that effort looks like it will go to waste or knock me off of my own course in life.

Why would you ever want to date someone who can't keep their own dating life and healing in order? If she's constantly being cheated on by the same men and runs back to them for more, then only hits you up when everything is going horribly wrong with those other men, what does that tell you about her ability to manage her own worth? What happens when she starts having sex with you until her ex comes back? What happens when you realize she was full of shit about all her stories of being abused and is actually just as manipulative as her exes and starts emotionally abusing you?

Don't put yourself in these types of situations. Women who are like this do not want to be saved. They want to continue behaving like this and playing the victim card. When they want things to change, they will change their focus away from men and onto themselves to heal. They are not yet emotionally mature enough to be in a relationship that can succeed. And YOU can't make them mature.

***the overall message -- resist putting your sanity on the line to save someone with self-caused problems -- This is a cautionary tale about a certain kind of manipulative person who repaints history to make themselves the victim. I never want victims of abuse to ever be discouraged by these words. Not all women who end up dating bad men are "of poor decision-making skills". Nor are all of them "full of shit" and "as manipulative as their exes". If the conversation arises about past issues about any form of abuse, a woman shouldn't have to feel like she must hide that just so a man doesn't think she is too damaged or secretly manipulative. This message is a warning to men about a very specific kind of woman.

I don't want abused people to think that they are garbage, unworthy of love, and not worth dating. The exact reason men want to save damaged women and end up getting hurt is the same reason many women date a damaged man and end up getting hurt. We are one in the same and it's a vicious cycle. We all want to stop someone from suffering the way we have and get closure for the pains of past relationships. I just want to make sure that you know that hurt people are not always vindictive monsters. Some hurt people are only wounded animals.

Fuckboyitis

When you don't love yourself, you attract others who don't love themselves like a contagious virus. You are what you choose to attract, and if you only attract fuckboys and fuckgirls, you may be infected. You whine about each other, but continue to drift towards each other based on shared insecurities and the ability to exploit those insecurities for personal satisfaction. The truth is, you subconsciously love what you say you hate. This refers to "soul ties": You are each other's type.

He is very manipulative and emotional; she is willing to deal with it. She always lies, and he is willing to believe it all. He is somehow always the victim, and she accepts the blame. You both have soft spots for each other because the REAL you is just as insecure and hurt as the other person.

You have this "fix them" nature to you. So, you entertain these type of people more than you avoid them. It seems like every time you try to date, it's with a fuckboy or fuckgirl. But WHYYY? Because it gives you an opportunity to "prove your worth, win them over and fix them" because you are a "natural giver" and you want to cure them of their Fuckboy or Fuckgirl mindset. You are so ready to give excuses for each other: "It's not their fault, they just got out of a bad relationship. They had a rough upbringing".

#DickWithStandards

Protect yourself. Condoms break. Plenty of women will be glad to suck you dry.... Literally - all of your Money, your possessions, your soul. Every woman doesn't deserve to be your potential baby's mother. That's all I'm saying. Some women won't mind distracting you from your goals as long as they accomplish theirs: To make a come up even if they have to make you cum... Up.

Free Single

Just because someone wants to be single and have casual, no strings attached sex doesn't mean that they want to play games with you. Respect the person who keeps it real the whole time and still chooses to be single. Yeah, they had sex with you for months but they also told you that you didn't have to stick around because they didn't want a relationship. It was up to you too, not just them. They'll let you know where they stand on not wanting a relationship and give you the option to take it or leave it. They give you that heads up because when they DO want to be in a relationship, they will want to give you 10000% for the reason that that's what you may deserve, and that's what they would have the desire to give to you... when or if they feel it. But for now, they feel as though they can't give you a relationship and commitment because they want to also give the single life 10000%. They openly communicate to you that if they get into a relationship with you now, they'll still give into the desire for other people and THATS why they do not want a relationship. They want you AND the single life. Having a single life is their choice but giving your body to them after they have told you what's up is **your** choice.

What some single people wish you'd understand is that you can be an amazing person, but they just can't take things seriously with you right now because they love being single. It is not that they want to mess around with a shit load of other people, but they do not want to have any worries about hurting you when they are out at the club or hanging with their friends. You never know what could happen these days. After a few drinks, a couple sexy stares from someone on the other side of the room and next thing you know, they are back at the house having sex. Or, their friends just met a new friend of the opposite sex that tags along. Or their freaky ass lonely ex is back in town and they miss the sex, so they decide to hang out for some Netflix and chilling. They want to have sex with them and not be called a cheater. If they are official with you, it would be called cheating if they were to sleep with those other people. They don't want to be a cheater. Get it now?

People become **fuckboys/girls** once
they start lying and manipulating you
just to use you and keep you there...
once they start purposely making it
hard for you to move on and be happy,
and when they start leading you on
with false promises about commitment
and future benefits in order to trick
you into sacrificing your morals and
standards for them.

The woman who is sitting alone at the bar probably wants you to go talk with her. She is out alone tonight at a bar instead of a party or club, and **open** to meet interesting people.

Nowadays, most men believe that in order to be more successful with women they need to be an overly handsome and rich man who is obsess about his looks and flaunts his money rather than his personality.

Take care of your grooming but don't obsess over your looks. Get a job/career, but have healthy spending habits. Go out there, talk with women. Smile and say hello to a cute lady in a store. Start random conversations.

Develop inner confidence and charisma. It will be scary, but women are just as afraid.

The Friend Zone

"The Friend Zone" is an imaginary place.

You think that if you show platonic behavior to her, you will get romantic behavior from her. It doesn't necessarily work that easily. Platonic relationships start differently than romantic ones, and they progress differently. If you want a romantic relationship you have to be upfront and go for it in the beginning, instead of trying to sneak your way into their heart through "let's just be friends first". Take no shortcuts.

Men are "friend zoned" for the following reasons:

He thinks that treating someone well is a substitute for asking them out.

He doesn't ask women out; does not let them know he is interested in them in a romantic way.

He thinks being nice meant not letting women know how he REALLY feels and what he REALLY thinks.

He is so afraid of disagreeing because he thinks it'll make women like him less. He is afraid of letting her know that he wants her romantically because he thinks he might get rejected. So he waits for her to want the romance. This fear makes him incapable of exposing what he really wants.

He goes after the wrong women. He pursues women

who do not match with his REAL values, interests, and goals. He keeps trying to date women whom he doesn't fully click with because he's trying to be someone he's not.

He is not in touch with himself and his masculinity. Since he doesn't know much about his masculinity, women never feel the confidence and security.

His behavior doesn't show "I like you, I enjoy your company, I would love to take you out on a date, I am sexually attracted to you, I want to date you."

He fears going after the women he really wants to date, instead he settles for women who he isn't even sure he wanted a relationship with.

**The truth is,
dating someone
who doesn't possess
every quality you wish
for isn't the same thing
as settling for less.**

Knowing the essentials that you want in a partner and being flexible on the rest isn't "settling" for less. Being open to dating outside your type is not settling. Most of us understand that we're not going to get every single thing we want in life and it really is okay. Sometimes, sticking to your "type" is the issue. Usually because you don't feel the "spark" with any other types. But, not all "sparks" happen in the first meeting or few meetings. Some sparks grow over time without forcing anything. Sometimes, people who aren't your type are actually better for you. Try it. Instead of the 6'6" guy with the beard, try the 5'11" guy with long hair. Instead for thirsting after the Instagram model who drinks tea to promote waist trainers and teeth whitening kits, try the girl with 300 followers who wears glasses and posts pics of her eyebrows. Instead of limiting yourself to one race, one city, one state, open up to others. Try it. You never know. Most of the time, we end up with someone who isn't our type anyways.

What do people mean when they say that you deserve better?

- they really mean that they think that you are too good for them and they won't be able to keep up with your expectations. "I don't feel like I'm enough and I can't be in a relationship right now because of that."
- they believe that you are not compatible with them.
- they are not feeling the "LOVE" anymore and they are sorry about it.
- You have done a lot of things for them and they think that they can never repay you.
- It could be a possible sign that they don't want to step up and take responsibility.
- It could be a possible sign that they don't feel that there is enough (emotional) attraction and connection.
- It is often a cop out.

Here is my truth, when someone tells you that you deserve better, they are telling you to move on because they don't care enough to be better, they aren't confident enough to be better, or they don't know how to be better for you. When someone says that you deserve better than them it's like saying that they know what you deserve, but can't give it to you, don't know how to give it to you, or don't want to give it to you and that they will not put in the effort they "**KNOW**" you deserve. Listen.

Personally, I feel that I would rather hear "I can't give you what you want." I can accept that. All I have to do is reevaluate the whole relationship to see that they aren't lying. Consistency would tell me everything. Maybe what I want is too much for them, maybe I want too much. Or maybe they aren't trying hard enough. And if we have given it an honest try at compromising but it still didn't work, it is what it is and at least we tried. It's easier to accept it that way.

Dear "you deserve better" people,

A lot of times, people assume that "you deserve better" means "it's not you, it's me" or that it's a way to break up with someone or let them know that you are not interested. They believe that "you deserve better," makes it obvious that they just don't want to hurt your feelings by completely being honest and coming clean about not wanting to be with you anymore.

No, it does not **always** imply that they are ABSOLUTELY rejecting you. It can honestly mean that they believe that you deserve better even though **you** are the only person who can determine what you deserve. It's just what they think. I don't see how it would be a cop out if they truly believe that they aren't enough for you. Sometimes, it is very true: you DO deserve better.

They told you because they feel as though they lack what you want and it's a struggle for the both of you. So, they care enough to let you go BECAUSE they care about you. It's not always about "giving up" or "avoiding responsibility". Its showing consideration for your feelings and their own refusal to hurt you any longer. It's not always a cop out. Its fully accepting their own flaws and putting someone else's happiness before their own.

I gave someone the "you deserve better" line. You know why? She **did** deserve better. I wasn't willing to commit to her and she deserved someone who did. Why would anyone want their partner to stay out of pity?

But, at the end of the day, it simply means exactly what they are saying; that they think you deserve better! Most times, there is no need to concentrate so hard on finding the hidden meaning behind their words, as if everything they say has a meaning other than the one the words literally convey.

When someone
tells you that
they will
hurt you, they
will
hurt you.
I don't
think they are
cruel or evil.
They aren't
planning
some massive
destruction...
but they are
trying to save
you from one.

We can only be
controlled as
long as we don't
care to break free

253

I AM THE LOVE OF MY LIFE

Manipulators Loves Company

Dear misery,

Misery isolates you like "I don't know why you're listening to your single friends that can't find a relationship even if their life depended on it." They attempt to bring you down and break you away from friends simply because they want your company with no one else there to change your mind. They quarantine you. They know that if you listen to your friends, you will wake up and know your worth and leave. But, it's so much easier to control you if the only person you'll listen to is THEM: the manipulator.

Misery loves company and you are that company.

It's sad because the distance between you and your friends actually reinforce the "misery loves company" saying. You'll think they are jealous of your relationship but in reality, they just can't recognize the person you've become, so they avoid you. But you think they avoid you because they don't like you.... NO, they just don't like who you're becoming with the person you're dating! You are dating misery!!!

What Is A Situationship

People aren't even dating anymore, just talking, catching feelings, sleeping together and ending up in SITUATIONSHIPS.

What Is A Situationship?

A Situationship is an entertaining, but complicated in-between phase of being more than friends with benefits. It is an arrangement where you are less than official relationship partners and you do not have a title, you do not know what you really are to each other; where two people haven't committed to being anything official for who knows what reasons.

You have sex, think that it is official when it is unofficial, not ready for a relationship, but ready to ACT like it is a relationship, messing around with someone for months or years who can only "see you in their future", but keep giving excuses for why they won't settle down with you, situation ship that sink. All because we allow people to treat us like they own us, without giving us a title or commitment. We allow them to get used to that arrangement. As a result, they see no point in "leveling up" to an official relationship.

Situationships are confusing and superficial. They seem to be laid-back substitutions for

255

relationships because you get the relationship benefits, but you also get to maintain your "singleness." Believing that you get the "best" of both worlds is exactly why Situationships get complicated.

Landing Into Situationships

When you mess around with someone who clearly wants to have you locked down while they are "free", intuition should kick in to tell you that that person is someone who most likely wants to have their cake and eat it too. That person is someone who can't, undecided or refuse to take ownership and be honest with what exactly the two of you are doing, out of fear that they may lose a good thing, and that good thing being you doing what they want. It's contradictory to then say you don't want anything serious but acting like you do.

So, let's say you have been seeing someone for 8 months now. It has never been an exclusive relationship but, you told them that you didn't want to see anyone else and they told you that they didn't want to see anyone else either. It started as "talking and texting", then friends, then became friends with benefits and has dramatically progressed into "basically a relationship" with no title, no commitment, no obligation, no responsibility with "no time for a relationship".

You were horny and so were they and you two had sex. Maybe because you wanted to test drive the car before you buy? You do damn near everything exactly as a couple would do but you really don't

256

know what you are to each other. And the confusion is ruining the "let just enjoy each other's time" phase.

Welcome to the Situationship life where bae isn't officially bae but it feels like they are. Where having some of a person is better than having none of a person. Where you get to have the benefits of a committed relationship without ever having to commit and still having a full and fun single life because at the end of the day, you can hide behind the "I don't want a relationship" loophole.

Situationships are so promising in the beginning for the "hopeful, one day soon he or she will be mine" person or for the "I just want to prove my worth" type of people. They believe that they can drive someone into wanting to commit if only they can "make them see" that a relationship would be worthwhile. And for a little while, they see things progressing.

Then, they spend more time and have more sex. They cook more and do more favors because they are "natural givers." They've finally found someone to fulfill their needs with supposedly no strings attached, while going with the flow, "seeing what happens" and enjoying each other's time because life is short and the future isn't guaranteed, so why focus on it?

On the outside it has all the distinctions of a committed relationship: similar interest, sex... lots of sex, chilling at each other's houses, dating, Netflix and chilling, effort to get to know each other through text messages, (possibly) meeting the parents and friends, and they may even argue like they're in a committed relationship. Yet, with all of that great penis and vagina clouding your judgement, it starts to feel like something is missing as if you're in the "going with the flow" phase for too long. But you swallow your concerns because you don't want to mess up what you have and you don't want to feel like you're pressuring anyone to commit to you.

Time goes by and there are still absolutely NO titles or clarity established, no rules, no regulations, no responsibility, NO BOUNDARIES! And suddenly everything just falls apart because you or the other person couldn't just "go with the flow" and enjoy the ride. It's usually too late by the time you realize it. Those emotions that you said you could control and hold back eventually catch up to you and slap you in the face. You're already deeply invested and months in without the "what are we" talk or commitment and the other person has already settled down with the no strings attached arrangement because that's all they signed up for.

"I don't want a relationship" loophole.

The idea of a relationship has become so watered down and infrequent because we are more individualistic, and anything that takes time and patience is considered a burden or waste of time.

A person can take you out, have sex with you almost every day, let you meet the friends and family, get you to stop talking to or dating anyone else, but when it comes time for them to have to do anything for you, they hide behind "I don't want a relationship."

They basically treat you like you are official, but when it comes time for them to stop talking to someone else, they tell you that you can't tell them what to do because "we're not in a relationship."

That's when you have to swallow your pride because it's true. You're not really together, and they know that you cannot hold them up to official relationship standards.

You're 100 percent single.

Why Situationships Fail

You get one part of the relationship -
but you don't get the heart-filled
benefits of building a life with
someone = short-changed.

Situationships fail because they are about the game of "who can fall last"; Who can NOT put in the most effort, who can hold feelings back the longest, who is going to ask the other person out, call first, or text first? The issue at hand is that there seems to be no real dating anymore, everyone is falling for each other, hooking up, and falling into a vicious cycle of, "We aren't, like, official or anything like that but we are hella cool and that's bae." But, every time you turn around, you still see a lot of hand-holding, touching, kissing, flirting, and more between a lot of people who are apparently not together. That's confusing for people who want commitment.

"Situationships" are confusing. The obvious uncertainty of your role or position in what is supposed to be a relationship drives you crazy. You don't know what the hell you are to each other. You don't know where it's going. You are not sure if you should just ignore your feelings or admit that you really like the person and that you want more. You don't actually know what they feel for you. You're often unsure about what you feel for them.

You are in denial. You claim that you do not want a relationship. You say that you want a best friend that you can sleep with, make love to, hustle with, go out with, shop with, basically live with. You just want someone who you can laugh with and chill with. You want somebody who you can trust and build with. Yo, what the hell is that? Isn't that basically a relationship without a commitment. You're in denial. You DO want a relationship, you just don't want to be held accountable for one and you don't want to take it seriously. Maybe you are afraid. Maybe you don't feel ready. I get that. But the issue is that you are unsure, and instead of trying to find out, you put your heart in harm's way.

You won't accept the truth. It smells like a relationship, it sort of looks like a relationship, and it may even feel like one, but is NOT a relationship. You just won't accept that it's not one fully. You can't keep holding single people who you chill with and fuck occasionally up to committed relationship standards. You are single as hell. You can't make anyone commit to you. They already see your worth. You are good enough, but you're not who they want to commit to. "I don't want a relationship" always means "I don't want a relationship." You're still going to be confused because you are not together, but have official emotions for each other. The longer you avoid accepting the truth, the more damaged you become.

Normal dating rules do not apply. There is no urgency to court you or ask to be courted and taken out on dates because "you don't want anything serious" remember? On any given day, the person can act like they are in a relationship, and then act single. And you can't really say too much about it because they are not committed to you, and you are not committed to them. So you say. You cannot actually hold them accountable for not following through with what they said they would do because there is no expectation to do it, they're not obligated to do it, they're not committed to doing it. No rules.

We don't appreciate the true value of a real relationship. We naturally take the easy route in every situation. So when it comes to commitment, it is so much easier not to feel like we are obligated to commit because of all the "hard" work it may require just to keep the relationship together. Wake up! Not much that comes easy is worth it.

You get to stop dating other people or playing the field. No more waiting for the phone to ring or receive a text. And no more laying in your bed thinking about how much you wish you were in a relationship. No, in a committed relationship you exchange insecurity for security. Uncertainty for plans and dedication. Confusion for promises. Being committed is working through the hard times. Being in a committed relationship teaches us that there is another way of seeing the world, to share, not be so self-centered... sharing the load, stress, worries, and frustrations of life, and having someone committed to help you deal with it all. You get to build a future with someone other than yourself. If commitment is for you, then date people who believe in it like you do.

You lied to each other. The person who doesn't want a relationship said that they did. The person who really wants a relationship said that they didn't.

Sometimes we mislead people, other times we misread people. There is always a situation where someone says one thing and the other misinterpret it as meaning something else. Someone can easily say that they do not want a relationship, but the other person assumes that they do, just because of the other person's actions (dates, sex, introducing them to the family etc.). They call it "treating someone like a girlfriend or boyfriend." But maybe, they are only treating you like they are simply attracted to you, and not like they want something more with you. Nevertheless, you read the signs a different way. They always say that actions speak louder than words, but sometimes, people misread those actions and ignore the words.

**Consistency reveals
how much you're
really feeling me**

Signs That You're In A Situationship

1. There is no title.
2. When you don't know if you're together officially or not.
3. If you've been going with the flow with no direction for more than 6 months while having sex.
4. All you do is text.
5. You consider yourself as more than a friend, but not officially a couple.
6. The sex is amazing... but so is the level of confusion.
7. *Fear of rejection:* If you never opened your mouth about wanting more, it usually never becomes more....
8. Someone is too busy to be serious, but always have time to chill and fuck.
9. No Commitment.
10. You've come to the conclusion that he/she isn't really the one but hey, "you'll hang with them now until someone better comes along"
11. No Obligations.
12. No Responsibilities.
13. No Accountability.
14. Someone can only "see you in their future".
15. You broke up with your ex and now in the "working on being friends again so that we can build back to a relationship" phase.
16. You are exclusive but not committed.

Friends With Benefits

Dear self,

"Friends with benefits" seem like today's ideal relationship: you have sex without having to deal with any "obligations"; meaning they aren't exclusively committed to each other and may not be emotionally intimate. For someone who doesn't really want to be in a relationship, but certainly wants to have sex, it starts off great. There are no games or agendas. There is nothing to prove and no aura of mystery and attractiveness you try to maintain. The main difference between fuck buddies or booty calls and friends with benefits is that for the most part, people in friends with benefits Situationships tend to value the friendship and not just the benefits. You are friends first, and as friends, you collaborate on something that is good for both of you without intentionally exploiting each other's weaknesses.

Friends with benefits work best when both people have mutual respect, similar expectations, and are willing to be flexible about change. It's awkward when one person wants a greater level of commitment, or becomes jealous of the other person's other options. The uncommitted nature of Friends with benefits situations also means that the relationship may dissolve at any time (in particular when one member wants to form an exclusive relationship with someone else) and this can be emotionally upsetting when someone was lied to or failed to communicate.

266

Being friends with benefits isn't "bad." They only fail when there's a lack of honesty and communication. Just like any other type of relationship. The lack of honesty and communication leads to confusion and insecurity, more arguments, more pettiness towards each other, a decrease in sexual satisfaction, and ultimately a decrease in gratification with the whole arrangement altogether. Therefore, it's not that friends with benefits situations are good or bad, it's all about how honest and open the people in them are.

Situationships:
Enjoying the fun parts of it.
Ignoring the bad parts of it.

Horacio Jones

no strings attached:

when you give yourself away

trusting another person

with your whole body,

but none of your heart

Horacio Jones

Committed Relationships VS. Friends With Benefits VS. Situationships

Committed Relationships

1. You have the title "boyfriend and girlfriend" with the actions to match or you have the stated and physical demonstration of "we are a couple". Although a title is important, it doesn't solely define a union. It only means something when the actions and commitment match.
2. Both people understand that being committed to someone in a relationship means they are NOT single and no longer available to anyone else.
3. There are only 2 people involved (usually). This provides stability, trust, security and safety.
4. They are both dedicated to building a foundation and to one day get married/stay committed to just each other and/or have a family.
5. They date each other, go with the flow with each other and enjoy each other's time.

Friends with benefits

1. You are friends first. Friends respect each other, and that means total honesty, more honesty than is required for a casual hookup, since secrets might cause problems that break the friendship. Friends help each other. Friends care for each other. Friends look out for each other's wellbeing.
2. You can genuinely have a great time with a *FEW* and *DEFINED* strings attached.
3. You *KNOW* "what it is".
4. Sex doesn't usually complicate things because of the high level of honesty, acceptance and communication with your friend.
5. You *can* break free and your friend usually *accepts* it without manipulating you to stay.
6. Both people understand that being friends with benefits with someone means they ARE single and ARE available to anyone else. But, they let each other KNOW when they date someone or have sex with someone else.
7. The friendship is more important than the sex.
8. You are sexual friends, who choose and consent, without having to lie.
9. You're not hoping to be together as a couple.
10. Sex makes you healthy and happy, and it's great for both people to choose that.
11. You're not concerned with hiding it. You *can* be honest with the closest people to you about what's going on.
12. Won't use sex with a friend in a way that your friend is being emotionally abused.

13. You're **not** ashamed of it, and you're having fun.

Situationships

1. You don't know what you are to each other.
2. Dating someone who tells you from day one they do not want a relationship and is not interested in any type of commitment.... But, they can chill and hangout to get to know you, go with the flow, enjoy each other's time and see what happens. And while things may seem like they are progressing toward something serious, they mostly never do.
3. You can genuinely have a great time without strings attached. But keep getting tied up.
4. There are no expectations.
5. You **claim** to know "what it is" but in reality there's no way to formally explain what's going on between you two because it hasn't been discussed or defined yet.
6. There's something in it for you other than love: sex, so you won't be lonely, just for entertainment.
7. Confusion mixed with sex allows the mind to put up with the lack of commitment because there's an addictive nature to it.
8. You don't know if you should break free to be fully single or wait for a commitment to be fully together.
9. You're hiding it. You can't be honest with the closest people to you about what's going on

because it's not socially acceptable and people will judge you for it.

10. You **are** ashamed of it, but you're having fun. So fuck it, right?

Every fuck-buddy has an expiration date.

Pros and Cons of Situationships and Friends with Benefits

Pros:

Company: You no longer have to go to the movies or dinner alone. You can call and vent to them and they'll listen or even come over later to "chill." You don't have to worry about being alone because they are willing to pay attention to you without you feeling the pressure of commitment.

A Trial Run at a Relationship: You can practice different dating methods without being held accountable for hurting someone when you want to opt out and date someone else. That way, if you want to embrace your inner "hoe" (male/female), you can practice with multiple people at once because technically you are "single."

You get to test drive the sex before you commit. Just in case the sexual compatibility is lame, you aren't obligated to stick around to work on it. You can just bounce and find someone else.

The more you date, the more you learn about the opposite sex. You find out what type of people you like and dislike. Maybe there are a few places that you want to experience things in a couple setting and with an unofficial lover, you can go... or not... you're not expected to follow through.

You are having amazing sex, so the other person will most likely tolerate you.

You even have the opportunity to learn what can make or break a relationship for you.

Sex: Who doesn't feel refreshed when the sex between you and your "friend" is amazing?

When we're putting the pieces back together after bad break ups, isn't the discovery of our newly single sexual selves a part of the process? Don't we want to enjoy the flirtation, the fantasy, and the sensation that comes from sex? Who doesn't love the jolt of energy and the boost to mood that comes with great sex? Don't we feel reassured when we re-engage with our sexual selves after a tough breakup? Yessir!!!!

Bae Magnet: sometimes, people who are in relationships (or look like they are taken) appear more attractive. Have you ever noticed that when you are completely single, it seems as though no one desires you... but as soon as you start heavily entertaining someone, ALL OF A SUDDEN people start coming out of nowhere trying to get a piece of you? Some people really want who they can't have and fall in love with the challenge of "taking you" from someone else. Therefore, Situationships create the "I'm taking" illusion.

The Real Thing: This is what most "oops, I caught strong feelings" people usually hope for: A Situationship upgrading to a REAL relationship with a commitment. In most cases, it is NOT a smooth transition even though you've built so much history and spent so much time together. The main reason why the transition may not be a smooth one is because someone almost always wants to keep things how they are NOW without the commitment because they weren't joking when they said that they didn't want a relationship. They have already settle down with the initial agreement of "no strings attached".

Cons:

Confusion: There will always be that elephant in the room: WHAT ARE WE.... REALLY? You don't know where it's going. You don't know if you should walk away. You don't know if you should stay. You are unsure about what they feel. You probably don't even know what YOU feel. You don't know if you need to plan a solo future or if you should include them.... You just don't know shit.

When you continue to go along with it even when you want more, you're showing the other person that you are okay with it. You are showing them that you will suck it up because you don't want to push them away. So, they continue to act like it's a relationship and let you obsess about "proving your worth" because they believe that they've made it clear that they didn't want anything more than "going with the flow."

Humiliation: After all of your effort to cook, clean, sex, chill, meet friends and family, pay for dates, buy gifts, and prove your worth, you find out that it wasn't enough to get a commitment. Not because you're not enough, but because they just don't want to commit no matter how great you are. Now you hate the person for "stringing you along" in a situation that YOU volunteered for. Then you have friends and family asking you what happened with your ex.... But that's not REALLY your ex.... And you don't want to admit that you were just a loyal booty call for all of those months.... Then you delete all the pics off your Instagram (but you leave that one picture uploaded). The whole thing turns out to be a big waste of time and embarrassing as hell.

Wasted Time: Self-explanatory. Lesson to learn: don't entertain what you don't want. Being the perfect mate but not getting what you wanted out of the situation for so long just reinforces your beliefs that you "don't have time" for a relationship because "people ain't shit" ... No... that wasn't even a real relationship and that arrangement wasn't shit.

You Probably Can't Hang

I don't think there is anything **wrong** with having a friend with benefits, but I do think you have to navigate it cautiously. Saying that friends with benefits can't possibly work for **YOU** doesn't mean that that kind of relationship is essentially damaging, "wrong" or "bad" — it just means that **YOU** and a lot of people who are engaging in these kinds of relationships aren't being honest with themselves or people aren't being honest with you. Maybe **you** just CAN'T handle these types of relationships. Maybe **you** couldn't abide by the rules of the friend with benefits situation, and that's why **YOU'RE** concluding that being friends with benefits is a bad thing. Sure, in that case for **YOU, it may be a "bad" thing**. That makes sense… for **YOU**.

I think a lot of other people enter into these arrangements thinking "well, I know that we are just chilling and going with the flow right now, but if we're casual long enough you will change your mind and want a real relationship if I prove my worth". But upgrading to an official relationship rarely happens these days because people just don't **listen**. If you both lay out clear boundaries at the start, and one person decides to ignore the other person's boundaries and hope for the best, then yes, they will likely end up hurt.

If you do not certainly want a "kinda single, kinda together" relationship — don't enter into one. It is not a stepping stone to anything but temporary fun and distraction from what you REALLY want… a **committed** relationship. But, if you do really want a friend with benefits relationship, then you must be willing to be an adult and discuss the terms. You must also be willing to remove yourself from the sexual aspect of your relationship if you begin to have unreciprocated effort and feelings (especially jealousy and confusion). A lot of people make friends with benefits work, but that doesn't mean it's possible for everyone. Maybe **YOU** just can't hang.

You don't always deserve the bullshit you put up with.

"Going With The Flow"

It's "just enjoying each other's time". It's taking what life gives you, rather than trying to mold a potential relationship to be exactly as you want it to be. It's the cool way of saying, "I really don't want to HAVE to try right now." Going with the flow sounds cool and all, but it usually feels like a way around dating *formally*. There isn't much thought or effort needed to be put in, which makes it the perfect exit strategy just in case it all fails. Instead of taking things seriously and having a plan, you get to wing it and if it all goes to shit, there is no feelings of failure…. you had no expectations because you really didn't try to take things seriously in the first place. ***Going with the flow*** doesn't actually fix the problem of "taking things too seriously and expectations always leading to disappointments," most times it's just a perfect way to opt out of taking someone seriously or a way not to have to care.

But I get it, life has taught us that we could be so sure about something that we "overdo it" too soon if any deviation of a plan comes our way. Strangely enough, the more we push, the more it runs away and the harder we make it on ourselves to truly enjoy someone. And even if we do have a good plan to build a relationship, sometimes the plan changes, the flow changes. Subsequently, we start to back up and "just let it happen" because we realize that we can't control everything and that maybe the flow can take us to a greater place together.

281

And of course, there are situations that are perfect for going with the flow. When you first meet someone, when you have no control of the situation. But I think that everything else needs a plan. It doesn't have to be too serious as if you're trying to get married TODAY. But at least have some sense of how you want things to go after months of "free flowing." Have a direction established.

It shouldn't be blindly drifting. It should be about awareness and creativity. The beautiful thing about the "flow" is that it feels natural... No pressure... No rules or boundaries... nothing serious... Freedom... But, the flow can take you ANYWHERE if you don't start taking it seriously after catching feelings for someone. The reality of the flow is that at some point, we have to grab the damn wheel and define, discuss, and communicate on where the hell this "flow" is going and if we even want to "flow" in the same direction going forward.

See, I'm the kind of person that needs explanations and clarification. I hate the feeling of uncertainty. But, I know things don't always work that way when you first meet someone and I don't want to scare anyone off by making them think that I am trying to rush them to commit or make promises. I don't want them to have to hit me with "let's slow down and just go with the flow", because I feel as though using "going with the flow" kills any conversations about actually being together in a real relationship. If you aren't having the conversations about a relationship, you're basically leaving everything up to chance. That never really works out. Does it?

Let's just be honest with ourselves and stop playing mind games. Instead of faking the casualness like, "I'm just going with the flow because expectations and titles complicate things," let's just say what it REALLY is, "I have no idea what we are, where we are going, if we are together, if I'm single, are you single, are we just chilling or dating, are we building to a relationship but I am just hoping for the best and whatever happens, happens... whatever that means." Yeah, it's a lot to say and NOT what you want to admit. But at least it's the truth.

My thing is this.... What's the point of being with someone unofficially – talking and having sex consistently, meeting family and friends, getting to know them physically and mentally – but not committing to it? Anything that doesn't have a commitment after a while is nothing more than friendship with benefits that's "flowing".

When you're committed, the flow continues but you promise to control the flow TOGETHER, you promise to take the flow seriously, and compromise so that you're both on the same page. That is when commitment = dedicated to each other and "Let's go with the flow and let it happen naturally" = no responsibility at all... No sense of urgency to date with a real purpose other than "fun." When it's just fun and casual, the only person grabbing the wheel of the flow is Jesus. But are you EVER going to take control of your dating life or always leave it up to the random ass wind currents like "whatever happens, happens?" You still don't know where the flow is going after 5 months? Are you fucking kidding me? You can't continue to give in to the fear of pushing someone away just because you decided to speak up for yourself upfront. And you can't let "I can see you in my future" have you waiting for something that doesn't exist.

Let's Just See What Happens

People suggest that you 'see what happens' instead of making firm plans because it's the easiest thing to do, and because everyone else is doing it. Therefore, it seems normal and convenient.

It means not to attempt to put a large amount of effort into actions and situations. And not to put much energy into analyzing where this bond is going, what these actions mean, what's the relationship title, where's the commitment, who else are you talking to, is this going anywhere, are we friends with benefits, just friends, are we dating officially etc. "Let's see what happens" and "let's go with the flow" and "let's just enjoy each other's time" all means not to have a particular goal, direction, or purpose with someone, and thus follow the majority while getting the benefits of a real relationship.

Know your worth...

I AM THE LOVE OF MY LIFE

People avoid relationships because they want to avoid the relationship drama, but get in Situationships and still deal with the same relationship drama

Futuristic Talk

What is **futuristic talk?** Futuristic talk is the load of bullshit that people spit from their mouths in the form of false promises. They paint this whole picture perfect future relationship with their words, they build up suspense, hope and faith, but never convert those words into actions. They talk about moving in together someday (even though you two aren't even in a relationship TODAY). They talk about having babies and raising a family (but you're not together today). They will tell you any and everything to make sure you keep your hope for "**someday**" alive and distract you from the fact that you haven't even gotten past level 1 of the current state of the relationship yet. You're on the "just getting to know each other" level 1, and they are talking about level 99 shit such as taking your family on a vacation and what would you two name your first son... the fuck? And when it's time to show up with the actions, they can say "**someday**" and there you go... gazing off in the "future" again... committed to a day that doesn't exist.

If you paint the future better than the present, people tend to lose sight of what's currently going on NOW because they've fallen in love with what "could be", while the present circumstances aren't as desirable or comfortable. When you fantasize, in that moment, you already have the things you want, so who cares about a mediocre, uncertain reality when the painted future is way more interesting to focus on? Reality has the best

287

face slap because the future doesn't exist. Eventually, you will have to wake up from that "I see their potential" spell.

Why do we fall for potential with "futuristic talk"?

Hurtful experiences will make you feel uncomfortable and motivate you to change, create a fantasy or try to get someone else to change so that you can see a better future. You would think that if someone was so obsessed with the future, they would commit to moving things and fixing things NOW, so that the future has a better chance of becoming real. But, it's sad to admit, some people are lazy or unmotivated to put in the current work because of how stressful it could be. They rather ignore what's going on **now** and just hope good shit falls in their lap. Or they wait for the other person to finally back up all of their promises.

When you fantasize about a better future, it makes you feel better. As a result, you may lose the motivation to change the current situations and allow that futuristic thinking to become a psychological pain reliever. Instead of instantly focusing on the current situation, you take the "I can see us together in the future" route and put off the effort for "the future". After a while, you get stuck in this cycle; instead of using fantasizing as a way to come up with a solution to the current problems, you let the fantasies become your reliever that you take every time you get hurt or overwhelmed.

I AM THE LOVE OF MY LIFE

Just remember this, the future doesn't exist. All you have is today. Potential will always be potential. Fantasies will always be better than reality. If you want to fix a relationship, both people need to start right now today.

Upfront

I choose to stay clear minded on what I want and anyone that doesn't line up with that will most likely have to go. Most people will feel some type of way and leave me alone. And that's ok because the average person does not understand that when you truly know who you are and have learned from your mistakes it's easy to block out what you know you <u>don't</u> want. It is easy to be upfront about what you <u>do</u> want.

I consider myself a deep person. I know myself. I want someone who is more than just interesting. I want someone who I could connect with mentally spiritually and emotionally because life has shown me that I can meet someone who is interesting and still not connect to their soul. Through my experiences, I've gained knowledge of the beauty of deeper connections. Anything less than that will not satisfy me.

I've had to accept that people are nice, thoughtful, interesting, have great careers, etc. but they do not always connect to my spirit. They're just not for me. The reactions I get to this conclusion is most often petty and sometimes harsh. They always say that I didn't give them a real chance or that I had "judged" them too soon blah, blah, blah. But on some real shit, I don't care. NO ONE knows what I want and need more than I do. I KNOW I will be able to identify that special person when they present themselves. Souls can recognize real. Truth

291

recognizes truth. When I find THAT, I'll stay interested. I am not picky or too stuck up. I am just very sure and upfront about what I want and I just KNOW that I want more than a fling, more than a lust.

Horacio Jones

The "What Are We" Question

It's all fun and games until someone wants to get serious. Talking, courting and dating is all fine until you try to label it and defined the direction for whatever it is that you're doing. All of a sudden, they "don't want anything serious; not ready for a relationship." How aren't you ready for a relationship if you've been negotiating "let's be exclusive" for months already? Whet???? You're not ready? It's been 200 days, 4,800 hours, and 288,000 seconds and you still don't know? REALLY? Are you even trying to decide?

If you're in that more-than-friends-but-less-than-officially-together stage, you're only human if you find yourself wondering about where things are going until you can't take it. Ex: You have been in the, "I don't know, but I like them," phase for months. Your feelings are becoming more intense. You already know the path that YOU want to take, so you finally ask "What are we?" because you want to know if you need to either invest more or fall back.

How DON'T they want a relationship after all of this time acting like they do? If only you had asked sooner, or believed them when they told you in the very beginning. The "what are we question" is one of our worst fears, and by waiting so long to seek clarity, we are only hurting ourselves.

Why is it such a feared question?

It is such a feared question because we want to know what they're thinking, and that's totally natural. But, at the same time, we remembered the last time we brought it up and it seem like it changed everything; they started to distance themselves. But, I want you to know that more often than not, any person who asks this question has most likely been trusting enough to share intimate "bonding" and HAS EVERY DAMNED RIGHT TO ASK their sex-mate just what the hell their confusing participation means.

See, I know that you do not want to rush it when you ask the question. But, at the same time, do you want to wait forever? I've found that the "What are we?" question can either make or break a relationship and that's why some people wait so long to ask it. We are afraid of the other person not wanting the same thing. *However, we have to understand that when it comes to relationships, both people are rarely ready at the exact same time. One person is usually ready before the other.*

It seems like people feel pressured when we ask them about the relationship status. But, you know it's not comfortable at all to sneak around in Situationships (more than friends but less than official relationship partners... confused) wondering "who or what or when" all the time while pretending that it is not bothering you because you want to keep the "peace". In my opinion, clarity is necessary. Without it, there's too much leeway and grey area allowed in that "we are not officially together" loop hole.

When Should I Bring It up?

Not too soon... ("too soon" is relative. What's too soon to you may not be too soon for others. It all depends on the feel of the bond you have with them) - No one wants to ask too early because they don't want to scare anyone off. When your instincts and common sense tell you it's time, it's time. Just ask!

Not too late... ("too late" is relative. What's too late to you may not be too late for others. It all depends on the feel of the bond you have with them) - Why wait so long to have big, important, meaningful discussions? You don't want to fall in love with someone then find out that you two aren't "long term compatible" or have serious plans that conflict with each other's. It's actually irresponsible to wait so long before talking about things that are honestly important to you.

That is why I think that we should ask when we know what we want. No sooner no later. If we already know what we want, why wait? We cannot allow fear of losing someone keep us in the "idk" phases while still fucking each other's brains out.

The Perfect Time To Ask

There's no magic day for when it's right to ask. We could wait 4 weeks (or 90 days □□□□) or wait until we've been on 6 dates. It's way better to listen to our own instincts and use our own judgment. For example, if we don't want to fool around and "chill", certain questions may need to come up earlier. **If we want to be more serious, it's time to bring it up while understanding that both people won't always be ready at the same time (yes, I am going to repeat this).** Bringing it up might get the person to step up or it might make them want to walk away... let them. As soon as we try to stay to prove our worth and try to convince them to crave dating the way that we want to date, we start to set ourselves up for failure because they already made it clear that they don't want what we want.

Therefore, it depends, when we feel that we have a good sense that things are getting serious, ask, not wait until the Situationship is already serious and comfortable for them. When we can tell that the "chilling" is definitely progressing, that's probably a good time to ask.

they are taken

a recurring theme in my life has been sympathetically entering someone's life when they were yearning for some help with grasping on tightly to the idea that they should let someone else go. i often become a supplement, their enlightenment, a catalyst for some insightful awakening within them that rewards them with just enough liveliness and mental strength to walk away and stay away.

it seems as though they always have someone stunting their growth and there I am... someone who shows them that there's more than what they are being given; that if they truly believe that they deserve better, they would have to leave.

you are welcome.

Horacio Jones

How To Build Trust

What is trust

Trust is a firm belief in the reliability, truth, ability, or strength of someone or something.

Trust is both emotional and logical. Emotionally, you expose your vulnerabilities to people, but believing they will not take advantage. Logically, you have evaluated the probabilities and pros and cons, calculating based on consistency level, and concluded that the person in question will most likely behave in a predictable way i.e. doing what they said they'd do because they have done it numerous times in the past.

Trust means that you have placed your confidence and faith in someone, and that you expect honesty, integrity, loyalty, and respect to be at the center of the relationship. You also expect them to keep promises and to stay with you when times get hard.

Trust is the willingness to rely on the actions/words of another person.

Trust Exaggerations

When someone says "I just don't trust you", it SOUNDS like they mean that they don't trust you AT ALL. But, in reality, trust is situation-specific. We actually trust someone to be able to do **some** things, but not **all** things.

For example, let's say you don't trust your lover with

relationship type things such as being honest and faithful. But, you still sleep next to them every night, you take them around your friends and family, and you eat their food. You even ride along with them when they drive. You don't trust them with being faithful to you, but you trust them with other things and in certain situations. You trust their driving, cooking, you trust they will not to kill you in your sleep. I hope.

It is important to understand that trust is situation-specific because focusing on some of those situations where you can and cannot trust them could help build, or rebuild trust. If we just say, "I can't trust you," there is nothing the other person can do to earn trust because we're saying that we don't trust them at all.

Also, saying "I don't trust you," clears us of any responsibility. But, when it comes to rebuilding trust or building trust, the responsibility is on both people not just the person who lost it. When we believe the other person is the source of the problem, and that the issue only will be resolved when THEY change, not much good can happen. Building anything in a relationship takes two people, a team.

Building Trust

1. Focus on yourself first, not the person you're trying to gain trust from. Why? Well, if you can trust yourself, other people can trust you too. If

you are consistent with things in your personal life, others can see that you can at least be a man or woman of your own word in your own world. Therefore, they get to witness your consistency with yourself in action. They get to watch you practice saying one thing, and living up to it for yourself. If you can take care of yourself, you'll make other people comfortable. If you love and work on yourself, people are more willing to trust you. They see the proof through your actions.

2. This is how I believe that consistency works: Let's compare it to Pavlov Dog Experiment:

Pavlov showed the existence of unconditioned response by presenting a dog with a bowl of food and measured saliva. He discovered that the dogs learnt to associate food with a new stimulus (bell) and would trigger the same response (saliva). The dogs had learned to associate the bowl and a bell with food after CONSISTENT presentations of both in SMALL lapses of time. Each time the dogs saw the food, they salivated. After pairing the bowl and bell with the food in short lapses of time, the dogs then started to salivate each time they heard the bell because they were used to food being presented shortly after. Because this response was learned (or conditioned), it is called a conditioned response. The neutral stimulus (Bell) had become a conditioned stimulus.

How does this relate to trust building? The dog

salivated when it had seen the bell or bowl because it had gotten used to receiving food shortly after (or at the same time). If people can get used to your words and actions matching, then they will more than likely start accepting them as two separate entities. For example, you say you're going to do something and then do it, people will get used to you proving it. Your words gain value when actions follow.

> Basically, if people get used to you being real, clear, consistent and upfront, they will learn to trust you again because they are USED to you proving shit. All you have to do is what you said you'll do. Make backing up your words a hobby. Make it something that you enjoy doing so that it all comes out as genuine.

She said I don't make her happy...

I don't want to be the only one in the relationship trying to make you happy, I want you to make yourself happy as well. I don't want to be the only one trying to love you. I want you to love yourself as well. I don't want to be the only one trying to put a smile on your face. I want you to look for reasons to smile more. Your life is yours... I'm simply in it. I am extra. Your happiness is yours... I just want to add to it, not be the only source for it. If you can love you better, you can love me better. And if I can love myself better for you, you can love yourself better for me. **WE** should be making you happy. **WE** should be making me happy.

Self-love creates winning teams...

You're Crazy

Are you "CRAZY", too sensitive, too emotional or TOO defensive? Are you always overreacting? Calm down. Stop freaking out. You're dramatic. Just get over it already. RELAX. Sound familiar?

Are you REALLY crazy? Hell no. But they keep calling you that over and over every time you get close to finding out the truth. "YOU'RE CRAZY". Sometimes, they call you delusional OR they hit you with "what the hell are you talking about?" As if they have NO CLUE.

The "You're Crazy Effect" is one of the best ways that **some** people hide their deceit these days. In **some** cases, you're REALLY acting far outside of your character and SEEM a little too dramatic. But in most cases, they just target your logic and emotions so that you can be re-routed away from whatever they are hiding.

Obsessive Truth Seekers

When you become obsessed with finding out the truth: Stalking, checking phones, social media, fake accounts, checking bank statement, stalking other people, being fake friendly with family and friends so that you can find out info, sending "mistake" texts, pretending that you are entertaining other people, breaking up just to see if they will chase you or miss you, lying about

303

trusting them, fake pregnant, fake ignore, fake busy... The person you're dating would most definitely start calling you crazy. You basically spend the whole relationship being petty and looking for the facts, making dramatic assumptions and STILL cannot find out what is really going on... so you stay with them because you haven't gathered enough physical evidence and you won't trust your intuition.

You can see how that behavior is considered to be "craziness" in some people's eyes. Yes, you need to calm the hell down. And yes, no one should take advantage of your mind. But, you can become so obsessed with finding out the truth that you push people away. Then when they start distancing themselves from you, you'll think it HAS to be because they are lying or cheating, but it may only be a matter of how they are reacting to your obsessive behavior. You may be doing wayyyyyy too much accusing, finger pointing, stalking and shade throwing. So, if you truly cannot trust someone that much, to the point where you have to stalk their whole life, maybe you need to exit the relationship?

If you have trust issues, that's **your** issue, first. That's yours to manage. When you feel anxious, like you NEED to stalk their exes, check their phone, hack their email, etc., stop and ask yourself what are you so afraid of, what are you so worried about? Getting cheated on? Being lied to? No matter how much stalking and investigating you do, you can't stop someone from lying and cheating.

If they have given you reasons to distrust them, then you need to manage that together. Did they cheat on you? Did they betray you? If yes, then why did you choose to stay, if staying means always being on edge? Does walking on eggshells work for you?

*** The thing is, when someone calls you crazy, they may be trying to make you second guess your intuition because you're getting too close to finding out the truth. But by pushing the blame onto your mental state, they can get off the hook easier without dealing with what's bothering you.

Unlearn Crazy Talk

Part of my journey towards becoming a better man was having to unlearn damaging habits. One of them was calling women "crazy" or "irrational". It's a habit that we men need to break; it's damaging to relationships and even causes mental health issues and – most importantly – hurts women. Now, she might not be crazy, but maybe she is tripping greatly and acting "out of character." But, that's not craziness; that's passion driven on a self-destructive path. She just needs to work on that serious issue within herself and calling her crazy will not help.

The truth is, when someone says that you're crazy, it's not always an example of petty behavior, it is often a manipulative technique call **gaslighting**, which is used to confuse people into thinking their reactions are so over the top that they MUST be overdramatizing and "crazy."

305

It is one of the world's greatest argument enders. As soon as someone throws out the "you're crazy" card, you are put on the self-justifying end, and instead of getting your point across, you start to focus on NOT looking crazy. If you hear it enough, you MAY start to doubt your intuition, emotions and mental state and instead start to only believe what someone else tells you to believe. You may start to question your own actions and feelings. It weakens your trust in your own point of views and you began to feel as though your opinions do not hold any weight, since they are based on being "too much in your feeling." As a result, you lose your identity.... you stop trusting your own logic. And now, you feel "crazy."

You're not
crazy.
You're just
in hell.
Your mind
is being
abused. And
I don't
know if
you've
noticed,
but hell
changes
you.

Manipulation
is abuse of
the mind.

We all tend to fall in
love with our ideas
of people before we
actually know them

The most important thing to realize
is that you already have a
relationship with yourself and that
this relationship is influencing all
the relationships you have with
others.

Horacio Jones

She wants him to commit,

When a man "catches feelings" for you and **wants** to be with you, and only you... he will show you and he would tell you. He would try his best to be consistent so that you won't doubt it at all. He does not want to leave room for confusion, insecurity, or even jealousy. If he has feelings for you **and** he wants to be with you, **and only you** it's almost as though no matter when you have sex with him, he's going to pursue more than just sex. He WANTS all of you. He **WANTS** to commit. He **DOESN'T want** anyone else. He is **WILLING** to make the required sacrifices and compromises in order to be with you and only you.

When a man has feelings for you, but does not want to be with only you, he will tell you that he doesn't want a relationship and proceed to treat you the way that you allow. After getting to know you and he still likes you but also still doesn't want to be in a relationship, the way he treats you is **NOT** preparation for a relationship, he is only treating you like he **likes** you. He will spend time with you because he likes you. He will have sex with you because he likes you. He would get jealous if you entertain another man because he likes you. He would do all sorts of things to show you that he likes you and enjoys your company, but that doesn't mean he wants to be with you. Especially if you tell him that you are okay with not being in a committed relationship. He enjoys your company, but doesn't want to commit to it because he doesn't **FEEL** it. It has more to do with HIS feelings, HIS character, HIS view of commitment and less about YOUR feelings and

309

behavior.

When he does not have feelings for you, it's all about the sex.

To know which man he is, analyze his consistency. If he wants you and only you and wants to commit, he will **TELL** you and **SHOW** you consistently. He will make it explicitly clear. If he likes you, but doesn't want to be committed, he will tell you but his actions will confuse you; his words and actions don't seem to match. If he only wants to fuck, his words and actions will always direct you to sex. There will be no dates. He won't be willing to spend money. He won't have time for you unless it's to "chill." He will disappear and randomly reappear. He mostly texts you. He has the best excuses for why he can't be with you.

Keep in mind, these things have to align:

he likes you
he WANTS to only be with you.
His morals decide if he wants to commit.
The life that he sees with you.
The way you make him feel. Do you bring peace or drain him of it?
You have to present your case and show him that he can't let you go. He can't get the benefits of a relationship without committing to only you. He can't wait too long to decide if he should make himself ready to be with you.

You are not going to wait forever. You are not going to act like his wife without the ring. You will not tolerate ambiguity. You add to his peace.

123456 MUST ALL BE ALIGNED

If 2 & 3 don't align, nothing else matter. His decision to commit has to be about his morals first and then your connection second.

Yes, some people will like you like crazy and STILL not want to commit to you simply because THEY don't WANT to be committed; THEY don't FEEL the urge to commit; THEY are already getting what they want from you without the commitment; they don't want to make the required compromises and sacrifices to uphold a commitment… but they love spending time with you and do not want you to be with anyone else. You can't make them WANT it.

Using Sex As A Weapon

Withholding - You can sit there and withhold sex from him if you want. But if you're going to withhold it (knowing damn well you want it too), do it because it is a practice of your religion, you want to wait until marriage, you don't know him enough, or you just don't feel ready. But if you're doing it just to get him to change his behavior or because you're trying to prevent getting played, it's not going to work because he will realize that you're using sex as an ultimatum, become uninterested in everything else, alter that behavior just to have sex, and when he gets it, he is going to go back to acting how to use the act... but of course "It all depends" on the guy.

DON'T refrain from sex as a punishment. When a man wants to commit, it's not because of how you regulate access to sex, it's because he simply wants to be with you regardless of the sex. Trust me when I tell you that while it might seem like a suitable ultimatum in the moment, withholding sex as a form of discipline will inevitably lead to more barriers! Using sex (or lack of sex) to express your anger is immature and can lead to resentment on both sides.

Think about it, sex is one of the best things that you two are compatible with; it connects you two; you agree on it. So, why would you take away the one thing that you two are compatible with? Sex isn't the issue.

DEAR RELATIONSHIP HOPPERS,

Make sure you want the person and not just a relationship. Sometimes, you're not in love, but you just **want** to be; you want all of the perks that come with being with someone; Sex, dates, gifts, trips, sex, food, sex and Instagram pictures and sex consistently.

You want the relationship life so desperately that you try to force people to fit it. Everyone has to meet the expectations of the "potential" that you're in love with. You want to be in a relationship so much that ANY person who pays attention to you is "your type."

Word of advice from a guy: A man who is thirsty for sex knows that a woman who is thirsty for any relationship will give in way before he ever has to. Meaning, he knows that he can get the benefits of a committed relationship way before and way more often without having to commit because you want the title, not him, and you're amplifying your "wife material" qualities to "prove your worth." You fall in love with "fixing" him which is a sign that you don't want HIM; you just want a man to fit your ideal version of a boyfriend, so you try molding the first guy who puts in effort.

Don't use a man just for the sake of having a boyfriend to post on social media or not to feel lonely. You'll get used every time. I hope you learn to love people and use things and not the other way around.

313

There are amazing people who try to be compassionate and empathetic of the someone's growth process and do not mind keeping things straightforward and simple in order to enjoy their company. But I've heard way too often that in most of these Situationships, someone begins to push "for the official relationship too soon" because the person who claimed that they didn't want anything serious brought it up FIRST. They say that they do not want a relationship but then are the first person to bring up relationship topics. Therefore, you begin to look at them in more of a future tense set of eyes instead of the present tense, then you begin to want to work towards that. But suddenly, they begin to back out and say things like: "you are a good person, but I need to work on myself..." They just get cold feet and start to back out right before things get serious and blame YOU for "wanting a relationship too soon."

Side Chicks And Side Dicks

We have all heard of the term "side chick" or "side dude." Those terms refer to secondary relationship partners that someone goes to when they are not with their "main" boyfriend or girlfriend, husband or wife. In most cases, the main partner is unaware of the side piece's existence. The problem with this side chick/side dude world is that its **cheating** BUT WE WONT CALL IT THAT. We make cheating look way to cute.

If you're having sex with someone else, and you know damn well they wouldn't be okay with it, you're cheating. If you're seeing someone that you know is in a relationship, you're helping them cheat. The way I see it, if you can't handle being committed to someone, then just don't be with them. If you feel the need to go to cheat, you should probably re-evaluate your relationship and whether or not it's right for you AND the other person. It's fine if you want to run through the city fucking everybody but don't do it if someone out there believes that you're fully committed to them.

Don't Be A User

1) you say that you do not want a relationship but you start bringing up relationship conversations. Why are you doing that? It's confusing. Stop it.

2) when they don't want to be friends with benefits anymore, you start lying to keep them there. They are your friend right? You care about them right? Then why are you lying and manipulating them?

3) you tell them that you want to be "exclusive" because you don't want them having sex with anyone else but YOU have sex with someone else. You aren't together officially but it will still feel like being cheated on.

trust issues

I hate the words "trust issues".
I do not have an issue with
trusting someone who is
trustworthy. I just can't seem
to trust someone who isn't
deserving of my trust. Whether
if it's because they've lied, or
because I don't know them yet,
Trust would not be an issue if
you're consistent, very
loyal and honest. I think
it can only be considered
a trust "issue" if you can't
trust trustworthy people.

@Horaciojones

I AM THE LOVE OF MY LIFE

Dear Self,

When hurt and broken down,
unhappiness and hopelessness take over,
life doesn't seem fair.

You don't feel loved,
You blame yourself
And pushed away
Family, lovers, and friends...
You feel lonely and worthless.

Dear Self,

When smiling and laughing,
happiness takes over,
destructive thoughts
go away.

You are worth it.
You are loved.
You are happy.

THOUGHTS

Somethings are meant to be for the present but not meant to last. Sometimes, love comes along to teach us lessons about relationships. We get to learn what we like and do not like about relationships. We don't know that it will be temporary initially, but eventually, we notice the benefits of leaving what's not making us happy.

We are destined to meet, but not always destined to stay in each other's lives. We fall in love and change each other's course of life. Sometimes for the better, sometimes for the worse... We become broken and learn the true value of rebuilding ourselves and loving ourselves... We learn that it's not about giving up, it's about acceptance, letting go and changing paths.

This isn't to make us bitter and resentful, it is to make us stronger. It is to prepare us for when love comes around again. And if we really learn what we are supposed to, love rewards us.

Now, we are ready. Now we know the value of commitment. Now we know the value of communication. Now we know the value of loving ourselves. Now we know what type of people we want to be and what type of people we want to be with. We were meant to cross paths, stop and laugh... Then let go of each other.

The thing is, sometimes we hold on too long or never let go. If you hold on too long to the person who is trying to leave, you may miss the new love that is trying to come your way. You run the risk of showing love that you are not ready for it. That you need another trial run full of lessons and unless you finally learn from them, you'll be trapped in the cycle of dating the same type of people until you learn how to stay your ass away from them.

I AM THE LOVE OF MY LIFE

The people you connect
with the most are mirrors.
They will be fake with you
because you are fake with yourself.
They won't appreciate you or respect
you if you won't appreciate or
respect yourself.

But

Your inner self is
your best mirror.

You are the best lover
you will ever have.

You are the only person
you can ensure will never
betray you.

Nurture your ability to
love and accept yourself
fully and the next person
you deeply connect with
will mirror that love.

I think we
can tell
a lot about
ourselves
by looking
at our
relationships.
Not just the
romantic ones
either. What
kind of people
do we tend to
attract? What
issues do
we typically
have with them?
It's more
likely an
indication of
the wounds
we are carrying
within
ourselves.

Horacio Jones

Don't ever attempt to upgrade someone who is only a downgrade for you. Help people on their journey, but never forget whose journey it is, **THEIRS**. Don't waste your time if the effort to help build someone else blocks you from your own course in life.

Horacio Jones

People will still continue to try to date you even after you tell them that you want to work on yourself. It is because they know that it is possible to better yourself while being with someone else.

Find someone who doesn't stunt your personal growth and who joins your journey and adds you to theirs.

Once you get into a relationship, you shouldn't stop working on yourself. You can continue to work on you AND the relationship.

You will always be work in progress and your relationship can be too. It's a matter of you being ready and willing to work on both. And being "ready" is not always a feeling, it can be a choice that you make and commit to

What's crazy is that,
when you stop giving
any ~~fucks~~, you become
the bad person because
you've turned "cold".
But, people don't
understand that when
you get thrown out into
the cold a few times,
you become a cold person.
And it's not like you do
it on purpose, it's just
a regular defensive
mechanism to keep yourself
from getting hurt again.
But, once that happens, it's
hard for ANYONE to change
back to how they use to be.
The problem with society
today is that they think
you're supposed to be the
same person no matter how
much ~~shit~~ you go through,
and that's where it's ~~fucked~~
up because it's impossible to
go back to who you used to be.
Whenever your heart and mind
is played with, ~~shit~~ changes

Horacio Jones

Relationships are voluntary.
We have a right to leave them
after giving it an HONEST try.
By all means, fight for who you
love. But when people don't
change, the feelings and
patience will

Horacio Jones

Lessons

"If you find yourself
dating the same type
of person, it's because
you have not learned
your lesson. Each time
you don't learn your
lesson, it returns and
will return again and
again until you learn...
Have awareness, know
yourself... if you truly
deserve better, choose
better."

Who you let go of doesn't always come back to
the same person. If you move on and grow,
and they DO choose to come back, they are
not coming back to WHO they LEFT. They are
running back to a better version of you who
seems attractive right now. They aren't coming
back to the YOU that they left, they are
running back to the YOU who won't settle for
less anymore. Remember that

- Horacio Jones

I AM THE LOVE OF MY LIFE

Self-love is a beautiful thing.
But, it's not the all-purpose
ingredient to eradicate the feeling
of loneliness. At times, you
and your *solitude,* comfort
zones, and *own space* are enough.
But, there **will** be lonely nights,
mornings and afternoons. That's
a sign: Your own love can get
lonely. And I think it's amazing
to have all of the self-love in the
world and still have this ability
to crave someone else's love.

Horacio Jones

We're often overwhelmed by love for someone else. And when things do not work out, we're overwhelmed by the lack of that love... And still, we find a way to keep moving. Loving yourself will continue to drive you forward when someone else stops. Remember that.

Horacio Jones

I AM THE LOVE OF MY LIFE

I believe that the purpose of a relationship/dating is to advance into the next level of getting to know someone EXCLUSIVELY. It seems as though most people nowadays get stuck in the "Let's get to know each other", "let's go with the flow", "be friends first" stages and never commit because they think that you have to know someone 100% before committing or that you have to become best friends before you commit. But, the point of the commitment is to continue getting to know that person EXCLUSIVELY after arriving at a point where you only want to see what you can build with that one person romantically.

Nowadays it just seem like people "mess around" but never make it to the real commitment because they get stuck "building a friendship" "going with the flow" "seeing what happens" and "enjoying each other's time" for months and months (sometimes years!) while having sex and doing things that committed couples do.

They think that they have to be best friends BEFORE they commit. They think that they have to know the person 100% before they commit. But I believe the REAL YOU comes out after you drop that commitment responsibility on that ass.

Think about it, most married and happy couples that you know today were not best friends before they got into a relationship. They became best friends during the relationship, right?

Think about it, it shouldn't take so long to know if you want to exclusively get to know someone. When you know who you want to get to know exclusively, you make a decision to commit to it. This doesn't mean you have to change your whole life in order to be with this person, it doesn't mean you have to start having sex with this person. Remember, you're still getting to know them, exclusively. The title doesn't have to be "boyfriend and girlfriend." I prefer simply saying "we are together officially. We are exclusively dating AND committed." This means, if someone else comes along who I'm attracted to and wants to date me, I will not date that person because I have already committed to getting to know someone else exclusively.

The issue is that most people are waiting years just to commit to getting to know ONE person exclusively. As months past, feelings grow, more time is spent, more sex is consented but no one is committed to it because "we're going with the flow, not ready for a relationship, seeing what happens, enjoying each other's time, being friends first." The truth is, you can still do all of that by making it blatantly clear that you're doing it with that one person.

What if the purpose of your relationship was to enjoy adventures with one person, spiritual growth and practicing commitment for marriage?

Door Closed

It is on you to keep the door closed after someone walks out. You can't stop or blame anyone who's trying to come back if you constantly leave the door unlocked for them. It's hard not to answer when you clearly
hear them knocking.

Thinking "maybe this time will be different."

But that's the same thing you said the last couple of times. You can't move on if you keep letting your ex flex on your progress.

Close the door.

Horacio Jones

You deserve
the type
of love
that you've
given.

One thing I hated
More than you
Was lying to myself.

Not So Sorry

How do we forgive the person we love, who has hurt us greatly but isn't sorry? I am personally not that good at forgiving people who have wronged me. I have learned that we should take our own time to actually arrive at forgiveness. Not force it. If you think about it, the concept of forgiveness is unpredictable by nature.

We usually read quotes about forgiveness, as to how forgiveness liberates us and gives us closure, which is true sometimes, but let's face it: It does not in any way reduce the degree of wrong done to us, nor does it help in everlastingly dealing with the hurt we feel inside.

We replay the situation in our heads over and over, trying to convince ourselves that we need to forgive others in order to move forward, so we rather appear to forgive because we feel it's the "right" thing to do. But, there are people who have betrayed me and I have not forgotten or forgiven and it is not causing me any pain now because I healed the part of me that was hurting and waiting for them to apologize.

In my opinion, forgiveness is an inside job which cannot and should not be rushed. You can't forgive someone unless you are ready with your whole being; mind, body and soul. After you submerge yourself in your work, exercising, healthy eating, friends and family, the wrong done to you will progressively become smaller with the passage of time.

Forgiveness comes with time.
Feelings come and go as waves...

Please remember to forgive yourself for the years your anxiety took away from you.

Remember, the paradise and the hell is in your head.

What you focus on, you make it your reality. If you focus on positive things, you create a paradise. If you focus on negative things, you create hell.

horaciojones

Convenience

Most of the things we do, we do them because they are convenient with seemingly small amounts of friction; little to no effort.

Amazingly, even if we want to change our lives because we're unhappy, we will still aim for what is easy and convenient, even though easy and convenience were the things that landed us here in the first place.

If you don't like the type of people you keep dating, why do you keep looking for the exact same type person in other people? Do you think that changing the person will make any difference?

Pause before you lie to yourself again.

If you do not like your relationships and the places or fashion you're meeting people in, why do you want to start a relationship in the exact same way in which you don't want to build in anymore?

Will aiming for what always seems convenient and easy really fix the next relationship if that method is what keeps putting you in the exact same situation over and over again?

Pause and think about it.

Only to be surprised that the new relationship

becomes the same relationship that you keep running away from.

I'm not suggesting that you look for someone you have to change or someone who is hard to be with. Look for someone totally new instead; someone who doesn't actually match your "type".

You can sit there and nearly beg someone to be more consistent with a particular thing and wait years for them to finally do it.... not realizing that they HAVE been very consistent.... With NOT doing what they said they'd do. Don't let "hope that they will change" blind you from the fact that when someone is inconsistent with one thing, they are very consistent with something else.

horacio jones

341

It may be impossible to ever meet the "perfect" person for you. You will probably never meet more than 0.02% of the total world's population. Statistically, you will live out your lives with someone who is tolerably compatible for you while someone who is a better fit may be out there with his/her "tolerable" partner. This is ok for me to accept because I am not looking for the perfect fit; I will not be looking for the better fit. I will choose to work to fit better with the one I already love.

The type of people who
pursue you are not always
reflections of who you are;
they are not always the reflection
of what you think you deserve.
We cannot deny how clever,
sneaky and deceptive some
people can be when pretending
to be someone they're not and
when pretending to care.

But who you choose
to stay and prove your worth
after constantly being lied to,
devalued and manipulated DOES
reflect what you think you deserve.

Staying is a choice.

Horacio Jones

343

everything
that I've ever
wanted to do
with you, you
wanted to do…
just with
someone else.

hj

Lies put holes in relationships. The more lies they tell, the deeper the holes they dig. At some point, you have to bury the relationship, not your feelings, not your worth.

Mixing lies and sex is just like mixing drinks... The only difference is that instead of a headache, your heart welcomes the hangover

Dear self,

The truth is, you will never find someone who can fill the missing pieces that can only come from within. If you still feel like something is missing, look inside. It's in there. If you do not see it, look deeper. Do not get discouraged; do not get distracted and don't change who you are for anyone else. It's wiser to lose someone over being who you are, than to keep them by being someone you're not. It is also easier to mend a broken heart, than it is to piece together a crushed identity. It's easier to fill an empty space in your heart where someone else used to be, than it is to fill the empty space inside yourself where YOU used to be. You are the love of your life.

I AM THE LOVE OF MY LIFE

When you prioritize,
you'll have a lot more
to bring to the table.

I got fed up with not being good
enough for you

Vulnerability is
an act of unmasking
to other humans the
whereabouts of the most
sacred and delicate
fragments of
my soul...

An excellent cure
for loneliness is
to travel

Sometimes,
saying it's "easier
said than done"
is an excuse for
not leaving when it
is necessary.

Heartbreak is a multidimensional monster. There are all kinds of **heartbreaks**.

Sometimes, you break your own heart.

Sometimes, some other person breaks your heart.

Here is a tip to help yourself move on:

Make a list of the things you stopped doing because of the **Heartbreaker** and get back to doing what made you happy before you met that person. Take advantage of your new freedom and submerge yourself in the hobbies and interests that you neglected while being in a relationship. That's a great place to start again.

Re-focusing...

Now, impress yourself. Set goals and achieve them.

Be different: If you want to stand out from all other men who are also trying to approach women, then you shouldn't constantly tell them how beautiful they are just because you want to impress them. Never put her on a **"I'm just telling you what you want to hear so you can like me"** pedestal, no matter how pretty she is! If you say it, mean it. Otherwise you're being a lame for lying.

You SHOULD be rejected.

Amazingly gorgeous women know that they are extremely attractive. They hear it every day. Every night.

Concentrate on **YOU** being stimulating and having an interesting conversation. Make sure **YOU** are comfortable. Make sure **YOU** are looking good and being the **REAL** you. That way, you increase the chances that she'll also be having a good time with you, falling for **YOU** (not your "potential") without you having to pretend to be someone else.

What is one of the biggest lies that society tells us?

"These are the best years of your life."

Just because you think that the middle school, high school or college years were the best years of your life, that doesn't mean that they're the best years of anyone else's life. It doesn't mean that after graduation, the fun has to stop. "These are the best years of your life" is a ruthless thing to tell someone who is going through a rough time during the so called "best time of your life" years. It's like you're telling them **things are never going to get better than this** and they should appreciate what they're currently going through only. It's said in such a way that makes it seem that as they get older, life WILL get worse. If you think that your **"young years"** are the only years you can have **"the best years of your life"**, you obviously haven't been to the nude beach or you haven't traveled. The "old" people are always letting it all hang out and still having fun. We should strive to make every year the "best year of our lives." That way, no matter how old we get, we'll still be having fun. I never want to have to constantly say "Things are getting worse. Ah... Life was good back in the day." I want life to be good today too.

If you want something, you have to prove that you're worthy of it. If you "deserve better," prove it by removing yourself from where you're not being appreciate and take it somewhere it will be treasured. You can't keep saying "I deserve better, I deserve more" if you're choosing to stay with someone who is giving you less; if you choose to settle for less. What sense does that make? No one owes you anything. Only YOU owe YOU at the beginning, middle and end of the day.

There are people who actually **choose** to be negative - **like, on purpose.**

This has been a very difficult thing for me to accept. I understand that there are people who end up momentarily in a negative space due to circumstances, and then have trouble pulling themselves out of it, but, there are people who truly enjoy being manipulative and negative.

Can you accept that you will never get answers to some questions?

If your answer is **"YES"**,

Why do you so desperately need **"closure"** from someone who left you with **"no answers"**?

No answer IS their answer.

And suddenly, YOU are the only thing keeping you from moving on...

Close Your Own Door

Although it was hard for me to accept, it certainly made me a better person:

I'm not destined for great things. But great things happen.

And that is perfectly ok with me. I work hard and when great thing happen, I'm proud of myself. But, when great things do not happen, even after putting in so much hard work, I accept it. I learn from it. I grow from it. And THAT, to me, is always great.

If you are one of those

"why are they always
checking for me? They are
nosey and jealous. Why do
they care so much about
what I'm doing? They wish
they could be me"

type of people or

"why is my ex still calling
and texting me? They
certainly still care about
me. They MUST miss me
and regret hurting me."

Here is a slap in the face:

Most people don't actually
care, they're just curious.

I admit that I am weak, insecure, jealous, vulnerable and even fragile at times. And most of *those times*, I feel truly human. Other times, I'm either being strong or pretending to be.

I want you to love me deeply but never more than you love yourself. Love me better by loving you better.

— Horacio Jones

I will always be changing emotions,

I won't always be happy. That is ok with me because it reminds me that the opposite is just as true: *I won't always be unhappy either.*

you want to know

"where is this going"
"what are we"

they tell you that you
are just going with the
flow; they do not want
to rush things.

But,

the truth is, direction is
more important than
speed

it must hurt
to know that

"I'm sorry"
"I miss you"
"I will change"

*No longer reopens
doors for you.*

I AM THE LOVE OF MY LIFE

I don't understand
how you can fear losing
someone so much
if you've never actually
had them in any of the ways
you've truly wanted them
other than sex.

you have spent enough
months with their ego,
pride,
lies,
ambiguity
and laziness
to forget what being
valued feels like

more than anything,
"you deserve better"
means that i want to
save you from myself.

it does not mean *"try harder
to change
my mind."*

allow people to have a temporary
presence in your life

let go when it is time.

your intuition knows when.

listen.

better love is coming your way.

But, you will not **see** it until you stop
looking for ways to "keep" a poisonous
ex as a "friend."

Letting go means ALL THE WAY.

Sometimes you have to
disagree with your heart.

Even when
it is easier said than done.

Choose to follow your mind
and your soul as well.

Not just the heart.

they say that they love you, but cannot be with you until they figure their life out. But they continue to call you. they continues to text you. they continue having sex with you and they do not want you to be with anyone else.

but, they "**still**" cannot be with your heart, just your body.

months and months later... **still**, they are not ready to be with you fully but expresses to you that they love you. need you, want your company, appreciate you, do not want anyone else and that they see you in their future.

this is where you must understand the difference between love and manipulation. the difference between someone who wants to be with you and someone who just wants your company. the difference between being loved and being used.

the difference between a sure person and a confused one. you may love that man or woman but you are certainly being strung along.

as a place holder...

knowing your worth isn't enough. you have to prove to yourself that you deserve better by walking away.

and staying away

I AM THE LOVE OF MY LIFE

i promise
self-love will come.
and when it comes,
people will fade away.

let them go.
let them remove themselves.
let them release themselves.

there will be no room
for anyone else's fake
love when you are *really*
loving yourself.

I cannot tell if we
are afraid of being
alone or afraid of never
being able to find
someone better.

it all looks the same.

I AM THE LOVE OF MY LIFE

some people are content with
settling for only half of you

I'm so tired of hearing
"do not get your hopes up".

I am
an optimist,
a lover,
a giver,
a dreamer...
a **hopeful** romantic

and hope makes me happy.

If things do not work out,
I do not get discouraged.
I look forward to the next
wave, the next blessing.

*The F**kboy's Girlfriend*

She supports him faithfully and emotionally. She wants to help him reach the potential she sees and wants to prove her worth to him so that she can receive the love she feels she deserves. She wants to help him find his strength to become the man he's always wanted to be. Her goal is to comfort him, bring him peace and liberate him from his painful **"crazy exes"** and sad upbringing.

But, what happens is that he becomes dependent on her to be his **"*bullshit*"** enabler. His crutch. She is what he falls on before he hits rock bottom. When he hurts her and KNOWS it is wrong, she sticks around, showing him that she'll tolerate his drama, insecurities and "brokenness" because she is his emotional crutch who wants to be his missing piece to cure his ***fuckboy*** ways. So, he benefits from letting her sell herself to him. Instead of getting stronger, he grows weaker, more manipulative and more attached to this woman. He won't "let" her leave. He won't "let" her grow. He won't "let" her move on. He "needs" her to be his emotional punching bag... slowly turning her into the inner demons that he refuse to deal with... then he abandons her for someone else.

Made in the USA
Coppell, TX
24 May 2020

26367779R00207